BRITISH RAILWAYS
ENGINE SHEDS

ISBN 1 871608 08 2

Published by
IRWELL PRESS
3, Durley Avenue, Pinner, Middlesex, HA5 1JQ

BRITISH RAILWAYS
ENGINE SHEDS

CHRIS HAWKINS, JOHN HOOPER
& GEORGE REEVE

BRITISH RAILWAYS

LONDON MIDLAND
MATTERS

IRWELL
PRESS

The L&NWR made use of a variety of machinery for both coal loading and ash disposal. In this regard it was a pioneer, though in the fine spidery nature of much of it little evidence can be found of the vast concrete monoliths to come. This is the coaler at Willesden, put up in 1920 at the cost of £7,000, which must have included a fair amount of track work. Whilst many of these early plants featured the heavy steel girdered 'tippler' the tower and bunker associated with it could be arranged in almost any flamboyant way imaginable.

National Railway Museum

CONTENTS

MAPS AND DIAGRAMS

The track plans have been reproduced at a uniform scale of approximately two chains to one inch in order to show the comparative sizes of locations. Drawings of structures have been reproduced at recognised modelling scales of 2, 3 and 4mm to one foot as space permits.

N°92

The '250 ton bunker' at Crewe South, the fourth mechanical installation (at least) made by the company. The L&NWR was moreover frequently associated with ash lifting plants and there is little doubt that development would have proceeded apace through the 1920s. That it did not, whilst the LNER forged ahead in such matters, must presumably be attributed to the Derby hegemony established upon the new LMS.

Mitchell Conveyor and Transporter Company

1. LOOKING BACK.

L&NWR experiments...Early Trials at Royston & Nuneaton...the first Modernisation

The four companies of the 1923 Grouping faced problems of organisation and change in widely different measure. The Southern, compact and farsighted, was assisted by a conviently smooth succession of officers in several critical spheres and transmuted its constituents into closely similar *Sections*. The LNER, similarly well placed, was content to operate more or less upon its pre-Grouping organisation, the constituent lines working fairly independently within three main *Areas*. Only a minimum of blood letting was necessary in the first year or two. The Great Western was untroubled by anything as grubby as this and simply mopped up the various (and variable) and hitherto fiercely independent, Welsh lines.

On the London Midland and Scottish Railway it was different. 'Opposing power centres waxed and waned' in the 1920s in a struggle for mastery and what became known as the Motive Power Department floundered amidst policy change and the cruder aspects of 'Midlandisation.' It is difficult to make rewarding comparisons between the Grouped companies-the 'Big Four' varied so greatly in their wealth and power and the means by which it was achieved. Each gained near-monopolies in belts of heavy industry and across major coalfields, most notably perhaps, that enjoyed by the GWR in South Wales. The LNER had the old empire of the North Eastern Railway

and the LMS (aside from some annoying ingress from the east) dominated transport out of the Lancashire coalfield. In the Midlands and Yorkshire there was competition between the LNER and LMS but it was eased and made increasingly comfortable by a web of operating and working agreements. In size and in the level of competition (there was a 'border' if you like, stretching the length of the country) and in the nature and proportion of the various traffics, the LMS was most closely comparable with the LNER. In the practice and organisation of engine sheds this (very) apparent similarity provides nevertheless for some fascinating contrasts and marked differences had emerged before 1923, in which the seeds of later developments can be discerned. Sheds on the English constituents of the LNER with the exception (at least in part) of the Great Central were marked by decay and poor standards of building, explained in the case of the Great Eastern by a general poverty and on the North Eastern, a prosperous line, by straightforward neglect. The English companies that were to make up the LMS however had evolved elaborate systems of standardised buildings, coal stages and layouts. The latest phase of new building had come in the 1880s and 1890s through to the turn of the century and although by 1923 the straight sheds of the Lancashire and Yorkshire and LNWR and the round-

L&YR 4-4-0 No. 1105 at Low Moor. The pre-Group sheds were striking, first of all for their neatness and relative cleanliness. Only through plentiful labour, cheap, preferably unorganised and subject to rigorous discipline could such a regime be maintained.

A. Davenport Collection

The Burton (Horninglow) 'coal hole'. This was the absolutely characteristic coaling means on the LMS, certainly until the 1930s. Even when sheds were *Modernized* many such structures remained as simple water tanks and a few were still in use for this original purpose until closure in the 1960s.

Collection K. Holden

Only on the LMS was ash *lifted* for subsequent dumping into wagons, a principle of working established, again, by the L&NWR. Elsewhere ash was always dumped, straight onto the ground or into pits (waterfilled or otherwise) for subsequent removal, either by hand or grab crane. The location is given simply as 'Crewe'.

Mitchell Conveyor and Transporter Company

houses of the Midland might show signs of wear, particularly in the roofs, there was not the dismal institutionalised decay found on the Great Northern, Great Eastern and so on. In Scotland sheds were built generally to a higher standard than in England though of the two principal Scottish rivals, the North British (LNER) and the Caledonian (LMS), dilapidation was possibly more apparent upon the former. By the mid-1920s an important LNER shed, take Cambridge or Ipswich, Sheffield Neepsend, Boston or Brunswick, was likely to be falling down and to date from the 1860s or before. Even the sober, often somnolent tones, of the various official Committee Minutes can raise a pitch or two at the condition of some buildings. Upon inspection of one wretched East Anglian establishment the LNER Engineer could use the term 'desperate' no less than three times. He plainly found the state of the place quite hair raising.

On the LMS there might be windows and doors and slates missing and important sheds were often very cramped and old (this was true of Camden though it did have a *mechanical coaler*) but in many instances the building would date from the 'nineties or later - twenty or thirty years old rather than sixty or more.

The interesting aspect of this situation is how the two companies dealt with their problems. The LNER was by far the worse-off for cash but embarked almost immediately upon a programme of investment in mechanical and other aids to the working of its steam locomotive depots. Each project was investigated and approved separately, to a strict budget and according to its 'strategic' worth within the scheme of things; March, York, Gorton and Doncaster are amongst the best examples.

Desperately short of cash the LNER was forced to concentrate each renewal project upon the best available machinery - coaling plant, wheel drops and on a simple form of water filled pit, where hot ashes could be dropped and slaked and thereafter retrieved for disposal. New shed buildings were provided in the direst circumstances but in many instances the slow decay had to continue. Despite its straits the LNER in its first decade had contrived the best equipped and laid out depots in the country, a small number as a proportion of the whole but increasing year by year.

The LMS, consumed by a prolonged power struggle, provided for a startling contrast. Odd developments had taken place, a mechanical coaler at Rowsley for instance, ordered by the Midland Railway and brought into use in the first days after Grouping. The Rowsley coaler was a presage of things to come, in that the main bunker was of ferro-concrete but its scale was to be dwarfed by subsequent units; the bunker type was not made standard for such medium sized depots; the Rowsley example proved in any case to be untrustworthy in its operation and steel framed 'elevators', first brought into use by the LNER, were purchased for the small yet busy sheds. But that is to leap on apace- with the company unsettled in the 1920s little of any note was accomplished, engines in the main got larger, a few coalers were put up on an early Bowen Cooke model of LNWR days (Royston, Wellingborough) and by 1930 concern was being expressed at the highest levels, under a regime bent upon exacting economies in every corner of its empire. Investigations and comparisons were made of disposal times and the relative periods spent by locomotives in traffic. A new shed at Royston was opened in response to changing patterns of traffic and it was carefully designed to eliminate the difficulties of cramped or ill-considered layouts.* Ample space was available (unusually) and Royston was built within its own triangle, its mechanical coaling and ash lifting devices placed so that engines might proceed from the running lines to be serviced, before running around the triangle (if turning was necessary) or reversing back on separate roads to gain the shed yard. Upon this streamlining of movement and the mechanisation of the heavy tasks, a small revolution was to be wrought.

Its operation- the movement of engines about the yard- saved hours in disposal and demonstrated, with some embarrassment, the primitive nature of existing layouts. It was a problem long ignored by the companies and only on the LNER, where North American principles first made themselves apparent in British engine shed practice, did it seriously begin to be confronted. The Southern too, stumbled on the economies waiting to be achieved, in the reconstruction of the old LSWR shed at Exmouth Junction (see British Railways Engine Sheds No2 - A Southern Style, Irwell Press 1989) but lost its way a bit with later

The L&NWR shed at Shrewsbury, neat and well ordered. It suffered a slow neglect throughout the LMS period, a situation unaltered under BR. Together with the equally decrepit GWR roundhouse alongside, it closed only in late 1967, a mouldering Webb remnant of the 1870s.

Collection B. Hilton

L & Y. R. — ACCRINGTON. — NEW ENGINE SHED.

The LMS (and BR) faced enormous problems with most of the varied sheds inherited from the pre-Grouping companies. This is Accrington, of the Lancashire and Yorkshire, in familiar northlight style. It is a fairly typical 19th century building, solid and executed with considerable craftsmanship but subject to harsh imperatives of cost. The contracts for such buildings were nevertheless detailed to the last nail and quality materials were specified: to an meticulousness which makes one wonder how the luckless contractor ever made money. Most of these buildings suffered considerable decay, not so much through their low roofs but through the very complexity of their construction. The roofs were a myriad assembly of bolts, nails, ties, glass, slate and wood - widely different materials which, imperfectly water-proofed and their maintenance neglected, soon deteriorated over the seasons. High up in the roof gulleys where leaves and sludge accumulated, rot, once it gained a hold spread inexorably. The wonder is that any survived until the 1930s, let alone the end of steam.

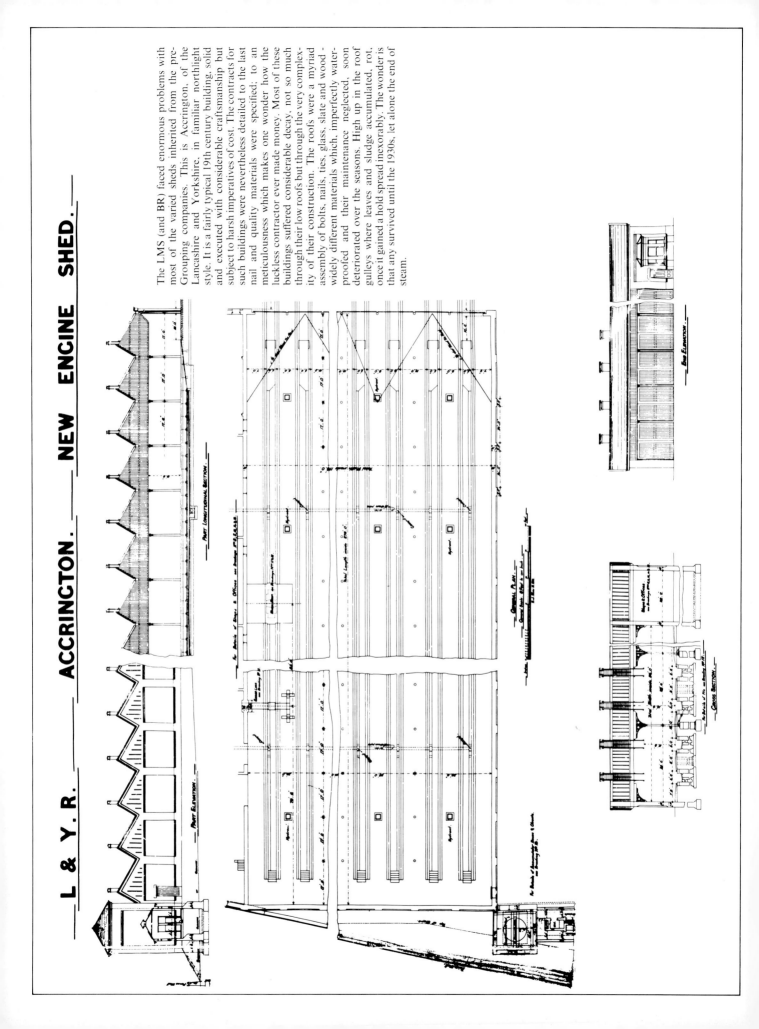

— Part Elevation. —

— Part Longitudinal Section. —

— General Plan. —

— End Elevation. —

— Cross Section. —

The 'ash carrier' at Willesden. Its crab-like framing was positioned precisely by the ash pit 'for maximum utility'and both fire and smokebox debris could simply be 'paddled' out into the iron tub for subsequent lifting. It transformed the deadening labour of ash loading but meant more shunting, nursing coal and ash wagons through the 'coal hole'. The little brick control room was standard fare for these installations.

Mitchell Conveyor and Transporter Company

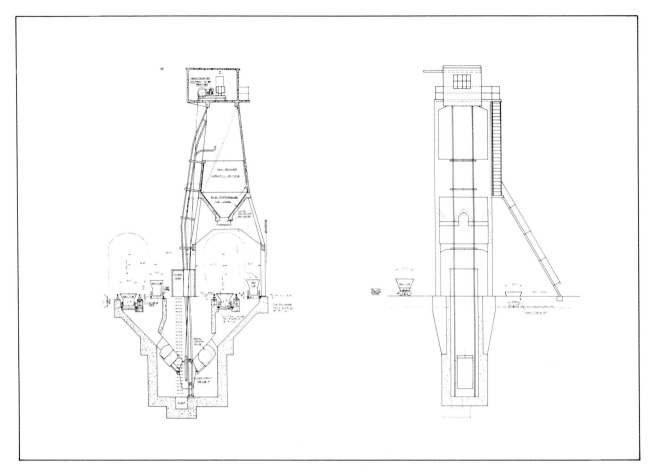

Later LMS ash plants, from the beginnings of the company's _Modernizations_ at Royston and Nuneaton, owed much to L&NWR practice in that the platforms were relatively lightly built, on a steel framing. The operation was more simple in that the motor was housed above and controlled by levers at ground level. These were much less obtrusive than later concrete versions and none now survive. This by way of contrast is the much later concrete ash tower, the type put up at Kirkby in Ashfield in the late 1950s. Despite its obvious refinement of design and sophistication of operation, its antecedents remain clear.

Mitchell Conveyor and Transporter Company

developments. The GWR remained content with its Churchward depots. To find that engines averaged less than 4½ hours 'actually working or assisting trains' was both startling and unnerving, made worse by disposal figures of six hours or more. 'Practice in the past appears to have been based on the assumption that the engine rosters constituted the final word'.

'Before Revolution must come Revelation' and Royston and some further schemes authorised in 1931 and 1932 provided this. The LMS determined upon the analytical approach to its troubles. It seemed to surpass the other companies in this regard, a reaction to the urgent need to drive down costs and (most important) the availability of Government finance. Maybe after the strife of the 1920s statistics and time/motion study provided for a useful independent 'arbiter'. 'Figures', then as now, have always had a conveniently incontestable quality. Peering across the Pennines at LNER activities, at the rearing up of the great concrete coaling plants, by a relatively poorer company, the LMS spluttered and started into activity with a handful of modest projects - amongst the first was Nuneaton authorised in 1932 but modified, almost as if 'cold feet' had begun to set in, within a few months:

'Traffic Committee 24th October 1934. Authority was given in 1932 for the Modernization of the Motive Power Depot at Nuneaton, at an estimated cost of £18913. This it has since proved possible to amend to £12614. This reduction has been made possible through:

1. A less expensive coaling plant has been provided.

2. Only one ash lifting plant has been built instead of the two originally envisaged.

3. In place of a sand drying plant the shed will be provided with dry sand from elsewhere.

4. Slight amendments were made to the plan for rearrangemennt of the locomotive yard.

5. The proposed mechanical smokebox ash extractor plant has not been installed (See later for the sorry end to this particular device, one of the few LMS mechanisations to prove an abject failure)

It was explained that the revised scheme was introduced on 19th December 1933. The mechanical coaling and ash lifting plants were tested and officially taken over and they are working satisfactorily'

Now the many engine shed _Modernizations_ of the LMS are certainly acknowledged to have been consistently the most comprehensive and far reaching; they were more widespread and thorough-going than that seen elsewhere in Britain. They are also the best documented, principally through the reporting of _The Railway Gazette_, culmiinating in a _Special Paper_ of 1936, arranged by the LMS authorities. This document has proved the basis of a number of accounts since (including _LMS Engine Sheds Vol 1, Wild Swan_, and has been reproduced in part or whole on several occasions since. It is now possible to enlarge upon many aspects of this classic description which in a sense has served its original publicity purpose almost too well, in that similar efforts made by the Southern and LNER (and pointedly not made by the GWR) have tended to become obscured. It is possible now to place the 'inauguration' of the LMS schemes (or at least the practical trial efforts) further back than 1933, the year given in LMS and _Railway Gazette_ reports and usually quoted since.

The coaler at Crewe South. In the early examples the trick was in the tipping of the wagons. Larger bunkers were necessary and most applications involved straightforward gravity, as at Edge Hill, where specifically bottom door wagons were shunted from an adjacent high embankment. More commonly the coal was emptied into a pit and lifted thence by belt or tub. The fewer the lifts (one big lift was preferable to twenty small ones) the more efficient the operation and Crewe South was one of the first applications of 'the big lift'. Once coal was in the main bunker, delivery was simply a question of gravity and minimal moving parts, with little power required.

Mitchell Conveyor and Transporter Company

The advantages to good shed layout began to dawn upon the LMS when Royston was completed in 1930. Wholly new sheds were unusual in Britain after the Great War and probably totalled no more than a few dozen if that, and then almost all were built with government cash. At Royston the Company was fortunate. A good site was available; in a district plagued by mining subsidence a triangle was deemed preferable to a turntable with its associated substantial foundations.'Cafeteria' principles were applied to the siting of the coal/ash plants with engines passing 'in forward movements from the time it enters the locomotive yard until it arrives in the road on which it is to be stabled or it leaves the shed yard again for traffic working. Improvements at Royston were indeed seen as dramatic. It had enough roads of relatively short length to ease the 'engine setting' problems (that is, making sure an engine was properly positioned for 'the off') and the new roof made for relative comfort in whatever fitting work was necessary. The shed was responsible for coal trains and shunting and little else and a 'unified complement', later notable as a concentration of 8F 2-8-0s, simplified the problem of myriad spare parts.

Collecton B. Matthews

It is clear now that the re-equipment and re-ordering of the LMS *Motive Power Depots* (a foreign term then, across much of the system) dawned in a small way around 1930/31, amidst a coming together of circumstances - the beginnings of a uniformity of purpose within the company, experience apparent on the neighbouring LNER and a regime responsive to technical means of cost cutting. The impression taking hold in later years has rather been one of a sudden coming into being of the various modernisations from 1933, following a few simple tests. Rather, the whole process was given careful trial, to be refined and developed as the benefits were realised. The mechanical plants in ferro concrete developed by 1935/36 and carried over into the London Midland Region of British Railways bore little resemblance to the first faltering and relatively flimsy apparatus. In addition the general principle of crews disposing their own engines was imposed (a revelation-see Nuneaton later, page 10') Opportunity was taken to put in place a locomotive supply scheme of Midland antecedents, the Motive Power Area Locomotive Supply, Concentration and Garage Scheme. It was not properly in place until 1935; some anomalies within it were never really sorted out and it was subsequently employed upon BR amidst some protest and to variable good purpose. Its ultimate expression came in the (abandoned) 'Line Allocation' scheme for diesel locomotives introduced by the London Midland Region, to

general scepticism elsewhere on BR. Its abandonment in ignominy was quiet satisfaction for the general imposition of a BR version of the 'Concentration and Garage Scheme' in 1950.

The LMS work then, sprang from an increased awareness of the economics of labour; it was afforded recognition and stature by scientific 'time and motion' analysis, eventually gathering pace enough to sweep all before it by the outbreak of the Second World War. To the original ideas of modernising each shed and the notion of the Concentration and Garage scheme was added an annual turntable renewal programme, new machine tool provision and the wholesale renewal of shed roofs, lighting and paving (though in truth 'renewal' was an inadequate term - the very walls of a shed had usually to be reduced by several feet back to the good masonry. Rebuilding would be a more accurate term, but less suited to budget and accounting considerations). On an undertaking of the scale of the LMS this soon became a vast irresistable rolling force descending upon one Motive Power Depot (the LMS habitually used the upper and lower case in this regard) after another and tearing it apart amidst a chaos of digging, scaffolding, works trains and rubble. Rather like the successive Gas Board/Electricity Board excavations of our roads, the turntable boys would arrive separately and the roofing firm would turn up months (or years) before or after to further scenes of apparent confusion. They usually contrived to eviscerate the shed with the roof off in its entirety in January; delays for the proper concrete work inevitably ensued, whilst the various gangs employed on the rearrangement of a shed yard would turn up in high summer, with movements at a maximum. Coal and ash plants were reared up in an impenetrable cage of scaffolding, growing to monstrous heights, amidst a confusion of debris.

Much of all this came to an abrupt halt in 1939, abandoned for lack of men and material. Work however gathered pace again from 1941 as the War economy pulsed and grew; with America entering the War a return to Europe became more than propaganda. The railways were taken steadily under closer and closer Government direction. Control was imposed officially almost at the outbreak of War, with the blessing and co-operation of the companies and it became further and further institutionalised as the conflict went on, until the railways acted more or less as a Department of State. The Ministry of War Transport had instructions to gear production for a peak of War effort in 1944 (as Churchill and Roosevelt indeed had promised Stalin, somewhat to his anger, for he had wanted 1943) and the railways were flayed to extremities of effort. The modernisation projects of the 1930s were ruled out - they demanded too much in labour and material and time and projects by definition had to demonstrate *a net advantage to the country by August 1944*. Projects with a worthwhile life decades beyond that were 'disallowed.' The LMS responded in good part to this and from 1940 established a continuing programme of war renewals - small (usually) but cheap and effective modifications; an ash pit here, a water column there to improve operating procedures at sheds. They had in the main been minor incumbrances borne with a shrug and a few moans pre-war but with the doubling and redoubling of work the remedying of them was to prove an irresistable advantage. Without waiting for Ministry approval of each project the LMS Board authorised a block grant on its own authority of first £50,000 and then £100,000 in order that the various renewals should proceed unhindered by any procedural delays. Progress was reviewed periodically by 'Special Report' and to read them now is to savour from far off something of 'bunker-Britain'.

Modernization **as the text relates brought a confusion of building work and whereas the term certainly included ash and coaling plant schemes, 're-roofing' could take place years before, or after. Such a site was Birkenhead, where LMS and GWR sheds lay alongside each other, with carefully duplicated yards. The LNW side had received a typical LMS 'single pitch' roof in the 1930s and was cut back in the process (the GWR position remained in the northlight style) but only 'unification' under BR allowed** *Modernization* **proper. The Western Region shed was formally 'made over to the Chester LMR District as from 1st January 1949' and the chaos of rebuilding, evident from these photographs, took place throughout much of 1955.**

G. Gilbert

2. 1933 AND ALL THAT.

'Experience gained'...some alarming figures...'The First Phase'

Official commitment of the LMS and its mighty resources to the wholesale modernisation of its engine sheds came on 24th May 1933, in a Minute of great moment:

Traffic Committee: Chief General Manager reported that the experience gained from certain of our main line running sheds, coupled with a detailed inqiry made by the special committee set up to consider the question throughout the system, had demonstrated that considerable advantages in operating efficiency are to be obtained:

(a) by improving the layout of shed yards and

(b) by the installation of mechanical coaling and ash disposal plants.

The main object is to ensure that the operations to be performed in connection with the disposal of an engine shall as far as possible be in forward movements from the time an engine enters the locomotive yard until it arrives on the road on which it is to be stabled or it leaves the shed yard again for traffic working. A diagram was submitted showing an ideal shed layout, the arrows indicating the course taken by locomotives going onto the shed and the numbered pink discs the sequence of the operations (this bizarre document is unfortunately long lost, though likely enough it formed the basis of The Railway Gazette's 'plan of a reorganised Motive Power Depot'. Generally thought to be an approximation of the layout at Camden, it has been reproduced once or twice since) *The Operations are:*

1. Watering

2. Coaling

3. Dropping Fire

4. Turning

5. Inspection prior to disposal in shed

These arrangements would permit of a much quicker turnaround of engines at sheds and result in engines being employed in actual traffic working to a greater extent than is possible at present and thus materially assist the reduction of the number required. In addition enginemen would be profitably employed for a greater portion of their time. It was explained that a comprehensive survey has been made of the position on the principal lines of the old London and North Western and North Staffordshire railways and it has been arranged that subject to the approval of the Chairman of the Board and of the Traffic Committee, schemes as and when ready, shall be immediately put in hand in anticipation of the approval of the Board, to be obtained at subsequent meetings as soon as the approximate and approved allocations of money respectively have been determined. Note - investigations which are being made also include consideration of the modernization of running shed machine tool equipment and schemes for effecting necessary improvements of this kind are being dealt with similarly to those having reference to the modernization of the shed yard layout etc. It was explained that schemes for the modernization of the layout of the depots at Rugby (L&NW) Aston (L&NW) Monument Lane (L&NW) and Lancaster (Mid), the latter providing for the closing down of the L&NW depot here, have been sanctioned in accordance with the procedure already outlined and these were submitted for confirmation. Particulars of the estimated costs and savings in connection therewith are set out below with approximate allocations in each case:

Shed	Cost	% return on expenditure
Rugby	*£13,990*	*9.4*
Aston	*£8,550*	*11.39*
Monument Lane	*£16,841*	*4.16*
Lancaster	*£2,024*	*51.87(!)*

The official account records that by 1938 'no fewer than 47 schemes have been authorised by the LMSR Board'. The expenditure by this time amounted to £750,000 'and the benefit to the company has already proved to be of a substantial order'.

After the new shed at Royston, the rearrangements at Nuneaton and some tinkerings elsewhere, new projects- 'Modernizations' - began to gather pace across the system. 'Outlay under the procedure determined by Minute of 24th May 1933' by April 1934 the following year amounted to more than £140,000

Depot	Total £	Return on Net Annual Saving £	Estimated Net % Outlay
Stoke	*17750*	*2269*	*12.78*
Derby	*25100*	*2352*	*9.37*
Leeds	*18690*	*905*	*4.84*
Peterborough	*11550*	*378*	*3.27*
Nottingham	*23200*	*1325*	*5.21*
Saltley	*22810*	*2960*	*12.98*
Grimesthorpe	*16440*	*684*	*4.16*

Later in the year, by October, further modernizations had been authorised amounting to £193,793:

Rugby
Aston
Monument Lane
Lancaster
Buxton
Edge Hill
Farnley Junction
Longsight
Patricroft
Springs Branch
Bescot
Walsall
Devons Road

This latest 'batch' brought once again the question of the additional economy that might be wrung from engine crews - see its initial surfacing at Nuneaton page xx. In May 1934 a second experiment had begun at Nuneaton 'the procedure of train enginemen completely disposing of their own engines after arrival at the shed, including coaling watering turning where necessary, cleaning of fires and stabling in the shed'. This has long been considered familiar routine at LMS sheds; hitherto it was asumed to have been age-old practice but apparently this was not so. The financial results of the new scheme were examined and checked after some months by the vaguely sinister 'Executive Investigation Office' though the findings were not clear cut. 'Based on summer working the annual net saving amounts to £2,050 but as the disposal arrangements have not yet operated during the winter months it is not possible at this stage to state what the annual saving will be.' The winter of 1934/5 at Nuneaton and the latest thirteen 'Schemes of Modernization' would determine if engine disposal was adopted as standard for footplate crews - it obviously was for this is the system passed down, with infinite local variations, to the end of steam. The revelation is that it was not institutionalised, apparently, until the 1930s. Of the thirteen schemes authorised in October 1934 it was expected...*that the estimated annual savings as now indicated are in respect of the procedure of train enginemen disposing their own engines after arrival on shed but when the various schemes are completed it is the intention where it is found practicable and economical to do so to adopt this revised procedure... although it is anticipated that this will be more than offset by further staff economy. The exact position cannot be determined until the individual schemes are completed and experience gained with the new procedure. If it is found that the suggested new procedure is found to be uneconomical it will be discontinued ...*

There seems to be no record of the footplate unions' response to this, whether they were opposed to 'the new procedure' or agreeable to it or whether they were asked, particularly. By November 1934 (it seems to have been the principal year for such matters) further schemes had been approved for Accrington, Agecroft, Bank Hall, Bedford, Bolton, Hasland, Holyhead, Lostock Hall, Low Moor, Lower Darwen, Mold Junction, Preston, Rose Grove and Tilbury with a further pair added on 27th November - Aintree and Goole. Without going into the sort of figures given on page 8 some of the estimated 'percentage returns on outlay' are startling - 21.42% at

Preston, 23% at Hasland, 23.77% at Tilbury and a staggering 36.6% at Holyhead. Others followed; Bristol ('put in hand from October 1937, £27,676'); Kentish Town, approved in October 1938 at a cost of £37,722 (work first began here in the autumn of 1933 with £6,544 expended on the closing of the repair shops substituting a wheeldrop for the old machinery; the modernisation of Springs Branch authorised in 1934 took place in 1935 and its final cost £17,707 was recorded in January 1939. The modernisation of Stockport Edgeley was recommended in March 1939, £12,852 with 'a net annual saving' reckoned at a less than startling £216. This paltry return as well as the threat of war through these months contrived to ensure that Edgeley would remain stubbornly in its LNWR state with 'coal hole,' handshovelled ash and particularly obdurate turntable, to the final months of BR steam.

The Railway Gazette's total of 47 'Modernizations' is difficult to track down precisely*; the term was fairly exact and meant only a rearranged yard with coal and/or ash handling apparatus. Turntable renewal, the concentration of machine tools and reroofings constituted separate programmes and whilst some sheds might be affected in all these regards (such as Newton Heath) more often than not one aspect or another was left undone. The LMS had considered repairs to the Midland roundhouses largely unnecessary; this task fell to British Railways along with many major unfinished depots such as Longsight and Wakefield in a 'Third Phase'(the terminology is elaborated below).

By September 1939 the Traffic Committee could declare a total authorised expenditure of £332,458** 'in connection with the Modernization of the following Motive Power Depots'.

Stoke
Derby
Leeds
Peterborough
Nottingham
Saltley
Sheffield Grimesthorpe
Huddersfield Hillhouse
Accrington
Agecroft
Bank Hall
Bedford
Bolton
Hasland
Holyhead
Lostock Hall
Low Moor
Lower Darwen
Mold Junction
Preston
Rose Grove
Tilbury
Aintree
Goole
Camden
Stafford

'The Chief General Manager reported that the actual expenditure incurred in these works is £371,043, an excess of £38,585.'

The Minute of 1933 provided the authority for all these schemes, the 'First Phase' if you like, of LMS shed modernizations. It was the most thoroughly comprehensive of three 'phases' which occupied the years 1929-1939, part of it at least dependent upon monies under the Government Loan Guarantee Scheme. The 'Second Phase' can be said to have occupied the War years, specialised and often relatively minor works, amendments (hinted at on page 9) to the most glaring problems as the War pressed ever harder. The 'Third Phase,' like the 'Second', little known and largely unsung, took place mainly in the BR period, from faltering, exhausted steps in 1945/46 to a late flowering of vast schemes on a scale to dwarf the work of the 1930s. LMS notions, spurred by its officers' observations in America and Europe, began to go into practice on other Regions, for the whole process to be brought to an abrupt end in the late 1950s. 1958 to 1960 saw the end of many things, great schemes curtailed, amended and finally abandoned.

The Gazette total seems to include Scotland; matters were very different on the Northern Division and were usually recorded separately in Northern Committee Minutes.

**'Modernizations' were costed separately from the other work and seem only to have formed rather more than half the official figure of £750,000

The steam engine shed had a quality of lighting and sound that was almost uniquely variable; 'the abode of dragons' turned sharply to nightime's warm embrace.

W.B. Underwood

3. HARD CASES.

'Lamentable problems'...Stoke and even worse

Carnforth Normanton and other problems ... too lamentable not too proceed forthwith.

Several of the *Motive Power Depots* presented such problems of dereliction and poor siting that only wholescale rebuilding could be contemplated. Carnforth is probably the best known and described, the locomotive department there labouring under the disadvantage of three separate sites:

27th April 1938. Carnforth. Proposed Modernization and improvement of former Furness Motive Power Depot and removal of former L&NWR and Midland Motive Power Depots. The Chief Operating Manager recommended that in order to permit of the concentration of whole of the motive power activities at Carnforth, at one depot, the old 'Furness' depot, be remodelled and extended and that the old 'L&NW' and 'Midland' sheds be demolished and the siding etc accommodation be removed. The scheme includes provisions of a No. 2 Type mechanical coaling plant, mechanical ash lifting plant, new water tank of 70,000 gallon capacity and water cranes, new 70ft turntable, electric lighting in shed and yard, modern repair shop, stores and office etc. accommodation and a new layout of the yard.

Under this scheme Carnforth would be the main depot in this District under the Area Locomotive Supply Concentration and Garage Scheme. The estimated sum to carry out the complete scheme is £71,571 representing a replacement in part only of the works to be displaced.

The carrying out of the scheme will enable 20 motive power staff and 3 signalmen to be dispensed with, the net annual saving being £670.

The new shed was indeed put up on the site of the Furness building but war brought severe delays; the turntable was in by 1940 but the depot was not officially opened until the end of 1944. Lost in state secrecy, censored reports and material and manpower shortage, the rest of the story is stolen from us by war; no detail is available to pierce these years at Carnforth.

Other special problems (a relative term if ever there was one and a condition which even the rolling Modernizations, re-roofing and re-tooling programmes were hard pressed to resolve) presented themselves in the 1930s. Normanton was an instance; authority had been obtained as far back as 1934 for negotiations to be opened with the 'L&NE Co.' .. 'with a view to the LM&S Co. taking over complete ownership and control of the joint LMS/LNE Motive Power Depot at Normanton as a preliminary to the Modernization of the depot, the L&NE Co. engines to be accommodated and dealt with by the LM&S Co. on terms to be agreed.' The Chief Operating Manager reported (this, six years later, on 30th April 1940) *..It had been tentatively agreed with the LN&E Co. the LM&S Co. shall, as from 1st October 1938 take over the L&NE Co.'s one third ownership of the existing depot on payment of a nominal sum of £1 (should such payment be necessary to meet legal requirements) and as from that date the L&NE Co.'s payments in respect of the use of the depot by their engines shall be in accordance with the normal reciprocal arrangements operating between the companies in cases where one uses, with its engines, the motive power accommodation of the other. The L&NE Board have approved this settlement and having regard to:*

(a) the desirability of our being asked to Modernize this important depot in accordance with our practice and

(b) the fact that unless we make a settlement of this kind with the L&NE Co. they will press a claim for reduction in the proportion of their expenses of the existing depot - which we might not be able to resist .. Recommended.

One of the principal reasons for taking over the L&NE Co.'s part ownership is to enable us to carry out at this important Motive Power Depot a Modernization Scheme on the lines of that carried out at similar depots. Normanton is situated on the old Midland line between Sheffield and Leeds and on the old L&Y Wakefield and Normanton line. The large marshalling depot at this place deals with the numerous collieries of the District and it is an important focal and exchange point for freight train services between the Midland and Central Divisions of the LM&S and the L&NE. *At this Motive Power Depot which is a garage under the Leeds main depot, 66 LM&S engines are allocated but although at one time the L&NE Co. made considerable use of the depot by their engines at the present time they have only an average of 3 stabled at the place. Existing layout at the Depot is not satisfactory resulting in considerable difficulty in the organising of the work and delay in the disposal of engines.*

It was therefore recommended that the Modernization Scheme be carried out at an estimated cost of £29,068. This improved layout includes mechanical coaling and ash lifting plants, water columns etc.

The Scheme would enable 5 coalmen and 3 sets of shed relief enginemen to be dispensed with and it is estimated that the saving in disposal time would equal approximately 30 mins/engine.

The work proceeded apace and the disposition of 'this important Motive Power Depot' was wholly changed. It had in reality been two sheds, backing onto each other, a Midland roundhouse of the' properly round, ancient Derby type' and an L&Y straight shed (actually put up by the Midland in its own distinctive style). Modernization obliterated the old roundhouse (of which no photographs appear to exist) and 'the 66 LM&S engines' were afterwards concentrated at the 'L&Y' shed.

Stoke was another notable case if only for the extremes of dereliction suffered there (though Leicester could better this doubtful distinction); the Chief General Operating Manager reported on 23rd November 1938, *that portions of the Stoke Motive Power Depot are situated on opposite sides of the main line, there being a Straight shed on the East side and a Round shed on the West side. The offices, stores, machine shop, staff amenities (which are unsatisfactry and inadequate) being adjacent to the Round shed. Considerable loss of time is involved as well as risk of accident by reason of the frequent necessity of staff to cross the 3 sets of lines to get from one shed to the other, in addition, there is the inconvenience and occupation of main lines by engines requiring to pass from one portion of the Depot to another.....*

The roof of the Round shed is in need of very extensive repairs, whilst the roof over one of the bays of the Straight shed was demolished some time ago for safety reasons. A renewal of the roofing at the Straight shed is a matter of urgency, strong complaints having been made by, and on behalf of, the staff with regard to conditions under which they have to work, especially in bad weather.

The main activities of the Motive Power Depot are at the Straight shed and, in the interests of economy and efficiency (economy and efficiency became almost an LMS slogan, a bit like strength through joy) *it is desirable that suitable offices, machine shop and staff amenities be provided in a convenient position in relation to the Straight shed.*

With a view therefore to putting the whole of the accommodation (including that for the staff) at the Stoke Motive Power Depot on a satisfactory footing and enabling the work to be concentrated at one, the Chief Operating Manager recommends:

1. The 'round' shed structure and certain buildings adjacent thereto to be removed; the turntable and lines radiating therefrom to be retained for engines stabling during busy periods; also that certain of the sidings be removed and some small p.w. alterations be carried out; other buildings in the vicinity of this shed to be placed in the hands of the estate department for letting.

2. The roof of one of the bays of the 'straight' shed to be renewed.

3. Altered and additional siding and pit accommodation are to be provided at the 'straight' shed.

4. A two-storey building to be constructed alongside the 'straight' shed comprising offices, stores, machine shop and general staff amenities.

5. A footbridge to be constructed over the traffic sidings giving access to the proposed new office block from Fenton Road.

Total Estimated Cost .. £22,117.

Conditions at Stoke by this time it is certainly true, were 'unsatisfactory and inadequate' (appallingly so - see for instance the series of illustrations in *LMS Engine Sheds Vol 4. Wild Swan*) and the LMS made something of a stab at rectifying matters. War brought it and

Hard Cases were not hard to find, they lay scattered about the system in somewhat embarrassing profusion and their renewal was frequently prompted by alarming incidents of falling debris - slates, glass panes and even more substantial parts of the roofing structure. This is Sowerby Bridge in October 1953, a Lancashire and Yorkshire Railway 'northlight' shed.

Yorkshire Post

Hard cases meant hard conditions and prompted (see later) a fairly pointless exercise to ascertain the precise percentage of BR sheds that were not 'watertight'. This is Goole in the 1950s, its famous office (again see later) on the left, built over the existing pit of No 1 road.

Leslie Tibble

much else to a halt and BR never properly took up the work again. The uncompleted portions of the work together with still-decaying untouched parts made Stoke a ruinous spectacle by the end, such to convince one visitor at least in the 1960s of the lingering effects of World War II bombing.

Longsight was a similar case, decay and ruin prolonged by War; like Stoke it had benefited from a 'Scheme of Modernization' belied by the tumbledown state of the buildings themselves. At Longsight the rebuilding proposals went back years; first authorised in 1933 and again in 1934, more than £18,000 was 'subsequently increased on the authority of the President,' to £19,076. Personal interest even of this elevated nature failed to secure any action and by February 1940 the Traffic Committee was bemoaning further dilapidation: *It was further reported that the existing roof of the 'South' shed is in very poor condition and as it cannot be economically reconditioned it is proposed to renew it in its entirety and opportunity taken to open up and recondition the engine pits on Nos 9 and 10 roads.*

Covered accommodation is no longer required at the 'North' shed (this

was a favourite solution to decayed roofing, inspired economy in a small way - the removal of a roof would certainly eliminate complaint as to its condition) *and it is therefore proposed that the roof and walls of this shed be removed except a small portion at the south west corner. Also that certain engine pits at and in connection with the 'North' shed and the shops be filled in.*
The foregoing and other incidental works are estimated at £52,725.

The LMS did not get a chance to put this neat forestallment of the *Luftwaffe* into practice and both parts of the shed, the 'North' and 'South' (or 'New' and 'Old' respectively) were eventually labourously rebuilt by British Railways. Leicester, Upperby, Crewe North and others were in equally deplorable state (see 'Case Histories' later) and illustrate in best fashion probably the whole story, from 'thirties dereliction to rebuilding on a scale then undreamed of - 'the full monty'.*

*An obscure phase - for its origins and meaning see later

Goole, a 'Lanky' shed fortuitously got rid of to the North Eastern Region. The northlight roof (see Accrington for instance, page 8) had deteriorated alarmingly by the 1930s and though the shed was *Modernized* by the LMS with coal and ash plants the company had simply cut back the front portion of the decaying roof, to leave a wind blown remnant, little better than an open yard.

N.E. Preedy

Holes in roofs, of the gaping sort, were in fact quite common - one of the worst was Brunswick in Liverpool (left) which the Eastern authorities were fortunate to cede to the London Midland and Rose Grove (below), a former L&YR shed which had once looked much like Goole and Sowerby Bridge. Its roof had been renewed in separate stages, in different styles. The earlier central part, of 'single pitch' type had fallen in, or maybe it burnt down, by 1956.
National Railway Museum

Buxton shed, close by the town yet surrounded (as the site is today) by open fields. It was thoroughly modernised with the earlier type of steel ash lifting plant and a concrete coal bunker; such combinations were common and the specifications which determined it can only be guessed at. Whilst LMS (and BR) roofs were remade in the so called 'single pitch' style, followed by the 'louvre' pattern, speaking very generally, an odd hybrid sort crept in. Presumably a specfic contractors design, for a closely similar arrangement was employed by the LNER at Cambridge and other places.

Collection E.M. Johnson

4. TURNTABLES, ROOFS AND THE LIKE.

Mundts and Vogeles...a colossal scheme...Kentish Town, Saltley, Bescot and others...a nice lunch

'Turntables and the like,' the Chief Operating Manager ordained would 'complement the various Modernization Schemes'. Each scheme, as we have seen, was strictly separate from any other new work which might be considered for a depot, and various features were only conjoined, it would seem, if an accident of timing made it so. Now doubtless if a Scheme of Modernization was under consideration and a depot laboured with a hopelessly inadequate turntable, then consideration might be given to its renewal but the Turntable Renewal Programme remained essentially separate. Bureaucratic problems seem to have dogged efforts to marry the two, which may reflect petty divisions within the LMS - the Renewal Programme had after all to accommodate new 'tables at sites other than Motive Power Depots and was of greater concern to the 'Operating People'. In addition a good many projects involved roundhouses where siting of the turntable was fixed, predetermining the disposition of ash and coal handling apparatus. On occasions the various programmes came nicely together but it was just as likely that a Scheme might suffer postponement or abandonment if the shortcomings of a particular 'table were of a severity to reduce the potential economies of the Scheme. It was really about getting the most for the money and all the components had to 'add up'.

New machines, offices, roof, water softener or whatever, all these programmes were run separately (in tandem might be a better description) and it is of interest to examine some aspects of this before

recording the war years ('A Second Phase') and the 'Third Phase' under British Railways. Without the separate programmes of the 1930s the great *Schemes of Modernization* would have remained relatively limited in effectiveness. 'Modernization' provided the broad brush strokes - a renewed layout equipped with the necessary mechanical ash and coal handling plant but the finer details of 'The First Phase' were slotted in as appropriate, or if funds were available. In this way the rebuilding and regeneration of the company's *Motive Power Depots* took place. The Turntable Renewal Programme was amongst the most obvious of the rebuilding schemes; it seems to have been inaugurated (or at least first thoughts were given to it) in 1932/3, soon becoming an annual process with the cost of each installation agreed and assigned to the programme for that year, presumably for reasons of accounting. For a turntable to be assigned to a particular programme did not necessarily determine the year of its installation - of the thirteen for instance which constituted the 1934 Programme, only twelve had been completed by the early part of 1936 and the last was finally abandoned: 'It was reported that the renewal of the 50ft diameter turntable at Manchester Victoria, Irwell Bridge .. involved considerable investigation with regard to the question of clearance with the adjoining lines whilst engines would be turning on the new turntable. The matter is being further looked into and in the circumstances it was recommended that the Scheme be withdrawn from the 1934 Engine Turntable Renewal Programme'. The first of the

43233 at Royston in 1957. Here from new the 'single pitch' roof characteristic of the LMS and LMR was first conceived.

Leslie Hewitson

19

Ransomes & Rapier undergirder turntable of 1931. This was fairly typical of the LMS at this period - it was often the largest that could be accommodated within a roundhouse, though it might be 'stretched' to 57ft or even 60ft.

RANSOMES & RAPIER
LIMITED.
ENGINEERS & MANUFACTURERS
32. VICTORIA STREET, LONDON S.W.I.

56155
55'-0" ENGINE TURNTABLE. OR. D4071/2.
GENERAL ARRANGEMENT.

47:3

The Ramsomes and Rapier 'table opposite could be found, with detail differences, amost everywhere on the LMS and the corresponding Cowans Sheldon products are hardly distinguishable. This is the Millhouses turntable which would presumably have been purchased by the Midland for the sheds opening, back in 1901.

P. Higginshaw

Millhouses detail. At 60ft it was the largest type employed by the Midland; introduced in 1900, they could normally only be placed outside. The great majority of Midland engines could turn on a 50ft 'table and all could use a 55ft one, so at 60ft the Midland was demonstrating a piece of foresight. The deep, centrally pivoting girder demanded fine balancing of course, eased only by a generous diameter.

G.B.Perkins

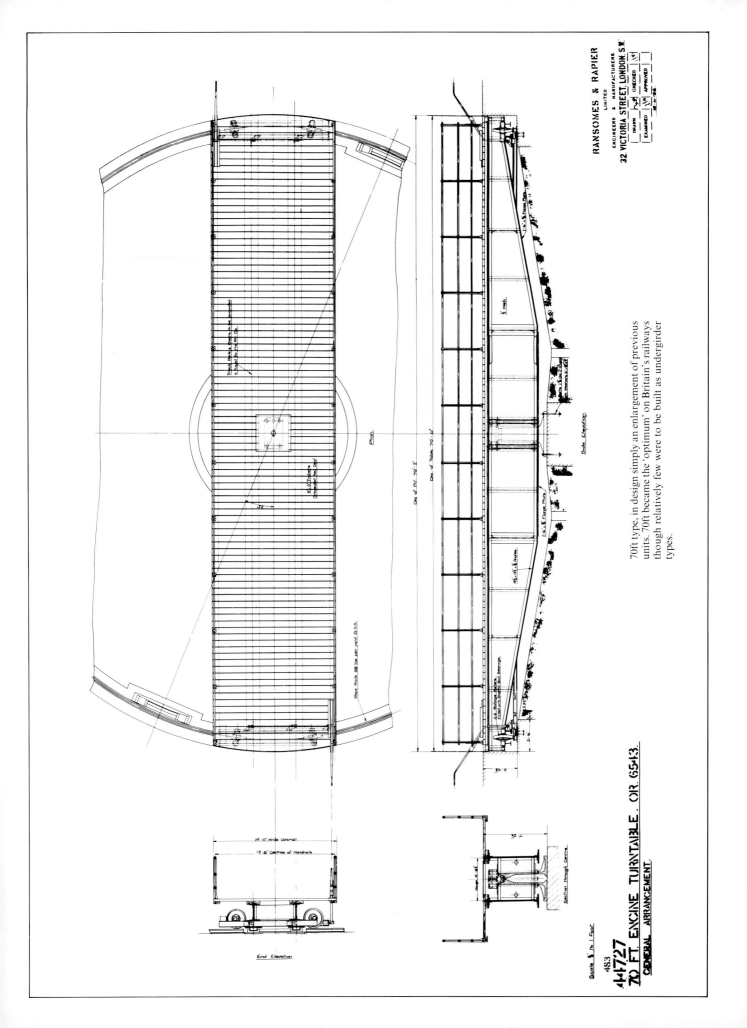

70ft type, in design simply an enlargement of previous units. 70ft became the 'optimum' on Britain's railways though relatively few were to be built as undergirder types.

Replacing the old undergirder turntable at Liverpool Central, an old CLC site, in 1952. The methodical, staged, approach and the problems are self evident. Turntable renewal on the London Midland had hardly recovered from the War; the Traffic Committee on 25th April 1942 explained that 'owing to difficulties in obtaining materials and priority licences work had not been proceeded with at eight of the authorised places - i.e. 8 out of 10 turntables in the 1942 programme. *Also under normal circumstances proposals would have been submitted for the renewal of a further 12 engine turntables but owing to the difficulty in purchasing the tables, the CME would keep 9 of these appliances in reasonable working order for the time being. In the circumstances recommendation was made that three turntables only be renewed and approval was given accordingly. The position in respect of the purchase of new engine turntables has now improved to some extent and as a number of existing turntables are in poor condition and in other cases are of insufficient size it is proposed to submit further renewal programmes from time to time. As a first installment it is proposed (a) that three engine turntables authorised in January 1940 be proceeded with:*

Cost	Location		Age	Dia	New Dia
£6,016	*Burton No.1*		*73*	*42ft*	*57ft*
£2,446	*Nottingham Eastcroft*		*43*	*42ft*	*60ft*
£5,076	*Normanton*		*60*	*50ft*	*60ft*

The Turntable Renewal Programme (presumably for 1945, for it was authorised on 21st December 1944) was reviewed on 11th July 1947 and further tables authorised at Crewe South, Derby North Staffs, Kyle of Lochalsh and Whitehaven. Later in the year the rest were finally tidied up:

Location	Age	Dia	New Dia
Aviemore	*50*	*55ft*	*60ft*
Belle Vue	*46*	*55ft*	*57ft*
Bournville	*53*	*50ft*	*57ft*
Helmsdale	*66*	*50ft*	*60ft*
Llandovery	*60*	*42ft*	*65ft*

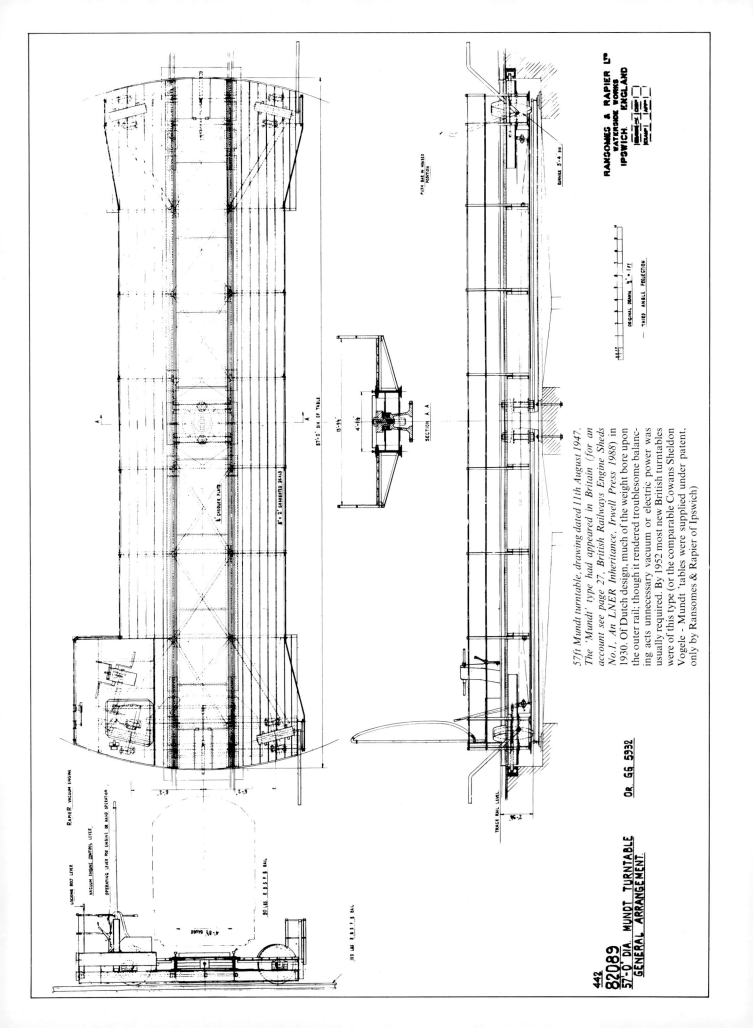

57ft Mundt turntable, drawing dated 11th August 1947. The 'Mundt' type had appeared in Britain (for an account see page 27, British Railways Engine Sheds No.1, An LNER Inheritance, Irwell Press 1988) in 1930. Of Dutch design, much of the weight bore upon the outer rail; though it rendered troublesome balancing acts unnecessary vacuum or electric power was usually required. By 1952 most new British turntables were of this type (or the comparable Cowans Sheldon Vogele - Mundt 'tables were supplied under patent, only by Ransomes & Rapier of Ipswich)

RANSOMES & RAPIER LTD
WATERSIDE WORKS
IPSWICH   ENGLAND

OR GG 5932

442
82089
57'-0 DIA. MUNDT TURNTABLE
GENERAL ARRANGEMENT.

The new Liverpool Central turntable was of the shallow girder type and thereby 'non-balancing'. Its makers plate proclaims John Boyd & Co. of Annan; with Vogele and Mundt the preserve of English firms, it is difficult to ascertain now the precise origins of its design. It looks to be 70ft diameter, which was by now regarded as standard: *22nd June 1948. Noted that the difference in cost between the installation of a 65ft and 70ft turntable appears to be generally not more than 10%. In view of the move to improve the interchange possibilities of locomotives, and the steps taken from time to time by bridge reconstruction and other works to clear the causes of restrictions on the bigger locomotives, the 70ft turntable (as previously notified) should be looked upon a standard wherever it is considered desirable or practicable to use a table of this size. It is appreciated that many factors need to be taken into consideration and that each case will have to be considered separately. The machines should be of the articulated three-point suspension type.......28th July 1948. The comparative advantages and disadvantages of electrically driven as against vacuum operated turntables were discussed. Noted that certain electrically driven turntables, of a type which required an operator other than the enginemen, have in the past been replaced by vacuum operated turntables to reduce staff costs. Whether electrically driven or vacuum operated, the type to be ultimately standardised upon must be of the unbalanced type, and not require an operator other than the enginemen (except in special circumstances). It was suggested that the maintenance costs of the electrically driven tables might be higher than the alternative type. To enable matter to be further considered with a view to a standard policy being laid down, agreed the comparative first costs, and maintenance costs of electrically driven and vacuum operated tables obtained..........1st March 1949. New turntables of larger sizes will all be fitted with an electric motor or be vacuum operated according to the merits at each depot concerned..........29th February 1950. Discussed, with particular relation to the Southern Region, the question as to whether, in the light of present day costs, 70ft turntables should continue to be looked upon when renewals are required. The Motive Power Committee is aware that the difference in cost between a 65ft and a 70ft turntable is in the region of £1,100 but nevertheless having regard to the points noted and the tendency to introduce locomotives with longer wheel bases, it adheres to the view that where space is available and no restricting influences, such as clearances, foundations to structures etc are present, 70ft turntables should be installed when renewals are required.*

1934 projects had been approved in May, a total of £23,880.

LOCATION	EXISTING	PROPOSED	COST
Stoke	42ft	60ft	4,000
Bank Hall	50ft	70ft	3,091
Manchester Vic Stn	50ft	70ft	6,799
Derby outside No.4	60ft	70ft	2,549
Gloucester Pass Stn	50ft	60ft	2,109
Gloucester Loco	50ft	55ft	2,257
Burton No.2	50ft	55ft	3,075

Two more were approved in July, Bath (46ft) and Llandudno (50ft) to be enlarged to 60ft and 70ft respectively at costs of £3,375 and £3,678, whilst £2,183 was authorised on 24th November 1934 to enlarge the 50ft 'table at Bedford to 60ft. The haphazard way of assigning projects makes it impossible to devine fully each annual programme. Fleetwood was completed in 1934 but belonged apparently to an earlier era: 'new 70ft turntable £3,414, replacing one of 50ft in a position which will fit in with a Scheme of Modernization of the Motive Power Depot. The new turntable has been installed, but cost £600 more than anticipated owing to piling having to be resorted to for the foundations'. Hellifield (50ft to 60ft, £2,276) and Manchester London Road (50ft to 70ft, £7,189) were authorised on 27th February 1935 and with that, further renewals pepper the Minutes in confusing fashion, amidst suspiciously agile juggling of cost allocations, referrals (and details) to all and sundry - 'a loose ball of accounting twine' is a subsequent description.

The whole lot begins to sort itself out by 1937, at least to some form recognisable to the non-initiate. In July 1937 reference is made to a Minute of 24th July 1935 authorising the renewal of twelve (all but two unnamed) engine turntables 'at an approximate outlay of £42,869 including provision for vacuum operated turning gear for each turntable and the acquisition of land at Mold Junction; the Chief Mechanical Engineer reports that the turntable at Canklow has not been provided with vacuum turning gear as the majority of the locomotives using this depot are not fitted with apparatus for creating a vacuum .. Estimated cost of whole scheme .. £40,365.'

The first unequivocal list comes in 1938, the last full 'Annual Programme' before war threw everything out of kelter: 'The 1938 Engine Turntable Renewal Programme amounts to ten, estimated to cost £42,643, each of the turntables to be of the articulated type and fitted with vacuum-operated turning gear, viz:

The Garage Scheme demanded a certain standard of machinery which was often lacking at quite major depots - the 'combination machine, incorporating lathe, shaper and drill' was intended to remedy most deficiencies; the idea was that every 'concentration' depot would possess such a thing or equivalent capacity but many anomalies remained. In pre-Grouping days and throughout much of the 1920s a great many sheds, ancient, ruinous or long stifled of traffic, might boast some sort of lifting capacity, usually in the form of shearlegs, handed down from elsewhere often and frequently built in wood. Given time and effort wheels could be taken out at most places across the system (even at such a shed as Lockerbie on the Caledonian). The Concentration and Garage Scheme demanded that many of these be declared redundant and where wheel sets needed to be removed then the task, it was ordained, should be accomplished with a wheeldrop. Now the pre-Grouping companies had thought to put these excellent machines into a number of engine sheds (usually precisely where the LMS did not want them); the LMS too installed them and a number of labourious transfers took place from 1937:

24th February: Chief Operating Manager recommended that with the approval of the Executive authority be given for displacement of shear legs at 35 undermentioned Motive Power Depots which are no longer being used owing to:
(a)unsatisfactory condition due to age
(b)limited lifting capacity
(c)introduction of Area Locomotive Supply Repair Concentration and Garage Scheme, whereby major running repairs are now only performed at the main depots and
(d)installation of wheel drops during recent years at the main depots:

Belle Vue (2 sets)	*Longsight*
Warrington	*Moor Row*
Patricroft	*Accrington*
Manningham	*Lostock Hall*
Leeds Copley Hill	*Aintree*
Southport	*Wigan*
Sutton Oak	*Stourton*
Grimesthorpe	*Millhouses*
Toton	*Peterborough*
Wellingborough	*Cricklewood*
Westhouses	*Mansfield*
Nottingham	*Abergavenny*

M.P.D.	AGE OF TURNTABLE	DIAMETER	PROPOSED	COST
Plodder Lane	51yrs	42ft	60ft	3,331
Widnes	51yrs	44ft	60ft	4,126
Keswick	78yrs	40ft	60ft	3,231
Wellingborough No.1	54yrs	55ft	60ft	6,076
Grimesthorpe	38yrs	60ft	60ft	4,397
Peterborough	37yrs	55ft	57ft	5,066
Toton No.3	39yrs	55ft	57ft	4,166
Evesham	69yrs	40ft	57ft	3,161
Leicester	34yrs	60ft	60ft	2,953
Liverpool Ex. Stn.	50yrs	50ft	55ft	6,136

Re-equipment with new machinery was a vital part of the LMS *Great Schemes*; apart from improved layouts, new roofs and coal/ash plants the Co. determined upon the 'provision of modern machinery for running repairs and a greater technical efficiency through competitive personal emulation, thereby reducing casualties,' a new repair organisation in effect, through the mechanism of the *'Area Supply Repair Concentration and Garage Scheme'*(see page xx)

'Personal emulation' manifested itself in the ill-starred 'Motive Power League .. 'thus bringing the staff into friendly rivalry on a competitive basis'. It did nothing of the sort of course but brought to full flowering every hitherto untapped seam of anarchy and deviousness. It was quietly done away with after a few years.

Bangor	*Swansea*
Rugby (2 sets)	*Bournville*
Bletchley	*Northampton*
Mold Junction	*Nuneaton*
Aston	*Bushbury*
Birkenhead	

A year or more later there was a further 'tidying up':
25th May 1938. Motive Power Depots .. Proposed transfer of wheel-drops etc. Chief Operating Manager and Chief Mechanical Engineer recommended as follows:

The Mundt turntable at Leicester in 1953 'shoehorned' into a pre-existing Midland pit.

The rebuilding of the Midland roundhouses required rather more complex solutions than the straight sheds, overcome by a system of beaming which to an extent replicated the earlier cast iron girdering. This is Cricklewood about 1948 though with experience at Leicester and Upperby it might have been easier to leave the centre open.

Dorman Long, City Leicester Museum

The former North British roundhouse at Carlisle Canal 'inherited' in a sense by the London Midland in the general ownership confusion of 1948/50. On 20th September 1948 it was determined that though it lay in the Scottish Region, its locomotives were to be replaced by LMR examples.

R.K. Coventry

4. TURNTABLES ROOFS AND THE LIKE

1.Additional expenditure of £520 in connection with transfer of wheeldrops from Nuneaton Bedford and Warrington, Edge Hill and Carstairs, estimated cost £3,208. Actual outlay, due to underestimate of costs amounts to £3,728 due to foundation work etc.

2.Expenditure on wheeldrops in authorised Schemes for Modernization of Motive Power Depots at Bank Hall and Nottingham to be lumped with other 'wheeldrop' schemes.

(a)Bank Hall. Existing wheel drop which was to be repositioned under the Approved scheme was not capable of dealing with complete engine bogies and the Vice President authorised its displacement and the transfer of a redundant wheeldrop from Nottingham .. £1,283.

(b)Nottingham (no details here) £2,285

3.Additional schemes for transfer of redundant wheel drops to Motive Power Depots where such equipment is still reqired from Royston to Barrow estimate £1,045. Staveley to Carnforth, estimate £1,087; Rose Grove to Newton Heath, estimate £995.
The total estimated outlay including the schemes already authorised amount to £10,423.

It is not clear to what extent the LMS made use of Government money, under the Development (Loan Guarantees and Grants Act) of 1929; that it did so is not in doubt but detailed references in the LMS Archive are not so far forthcoming* In its colossal drive to reduce costs and improve running performance (it involved an annual mileage of 230,000,000 at a charge of £12,000,000) it is hard to imagine the LMS spurning Government aid for the renewal of its depots but the recorded arrangements seem only to relate to staff amenity - just for this the astonishing sum of £240,000 had been put aside at least as early as 1935. It was devoted to the renewal of crumbling and leaking offices, mess and hostel accommodation, for their replacement was by no means cheap - at Blackpool for instance £30,000 was expended .. 'to be dealt with under the arrangements with the Treasury'. The existing hostel was declared to be 'totally inadequate in the busy season, therefore a new staff hostel should be provided containing 175 cubicles with the requisite amenities'. £2,400 was expended at Goole and £2,100 at Stafford in July 1937 for offices/mess including drying and washing rooms and lavatories. In 1938 a similar scheme for Nuneaton was costed at £11,198 and there were many more.

Of the last of such schemes before the outbreak of war (though it in turn brought different amenities - canteens especially) was Preston, where a new hostel was recommended at a cost of £12,907. The existing building it was remarked was 'an old mill converted for the purpose'. This was 'badly in need of repair and did not provide sufficient accommodation for requirements generally.' It was, the Traffic Committee attested somewhat sheepishly 'generally lacking in amenity'. With that the Meeting closed and doubtless adjourned for a very nice lunch.

though doubtless the details are hidden away in some as yet unexamined Minute Book.

Roundhouses were places of either an unnerving, eerie silence, or crashing tummult as the turntable flew about in scant regard of regulations. With smoke and gloom they could be places of wonder. Nottingham in the 1950s.

P. Hutchinson

Carnforth in the 1930s: the 'classic British roundhouse' was small, square and dated usually from the 1870s and 1880s. The LMS inherited a large number from the Midland and as engine sizes increased they proved increasingly inhibiting to the working of the traffic. 8Fs and 4-6-0s where they could be accommodated on the turntable, could only make use of the longer corner roads. Theoretically concentration depots, such as Cricklewood, ended up turning away Kentish Town (its supposed garage) Jubilees and Royal Scots, sending fitters down by bus or train on a daily basis.

W.A. Camwell

BR steel and glass, an effective and economical renewal of the Kentish Town 'No.1' roof.

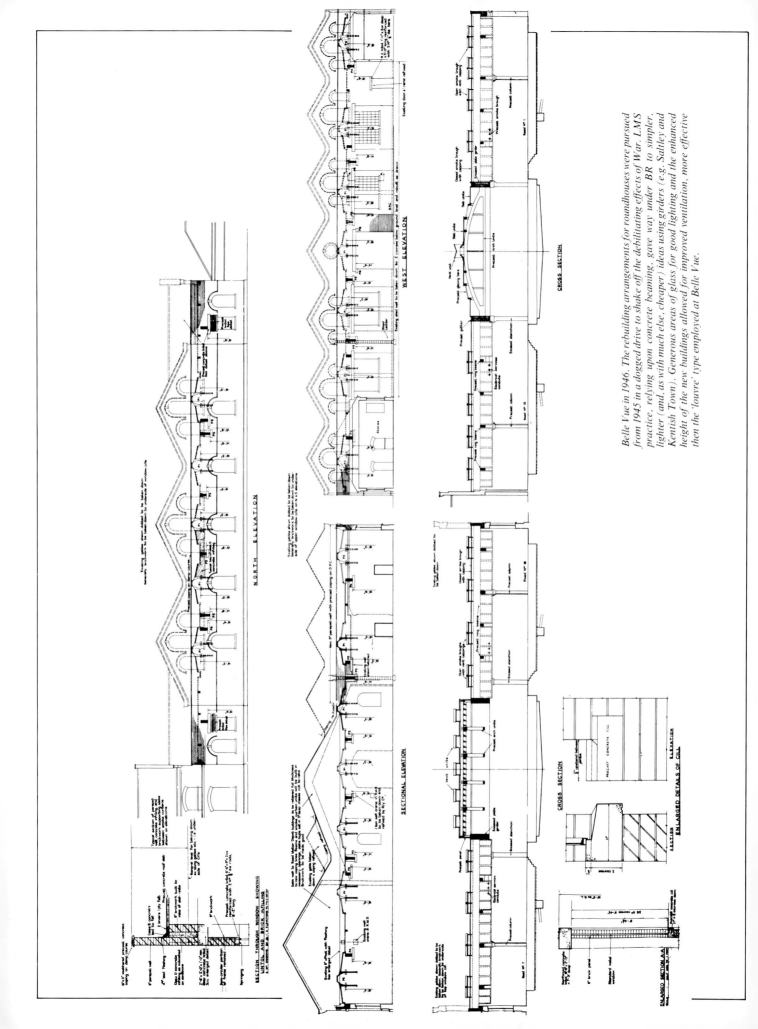

Belle Vue in 1946. The rebuilding arrangements for roundhouses were pursued from 1945 in a dogged drive to shake off the debilitating effects of War. LMS practice, relying upon concrete beaming, gave way under BR to simpler, lighter (and, as with much else, cheaper) ideas using girders (e.g. Saltley and Kentish Town). Generous areas of glass for good lighting and the enhanced height of the new buildings allowed for improved ventilation, more effective then the 'louvre' type employed at Belle Vue.

The Midland roundhouses survived well but when they were bad, they were bad. Saltley before its BR 'steel and glass' roof, in 1951.

H.C.Casserley

Stafford with louvre roof. 'Re-roofing frequently involved a loss of covered space; in the reconstruction of Stafford two old buildings made way for one and in many other cases (eg Accrington) parts of the original roof were cut back. This was a clever device; it was cheaper of course but did have some justification. Maintenance turnrounds and engine number declined throughout the time of the LMS and, it could be argued, less accommodation was needed.

R.K.Coventry

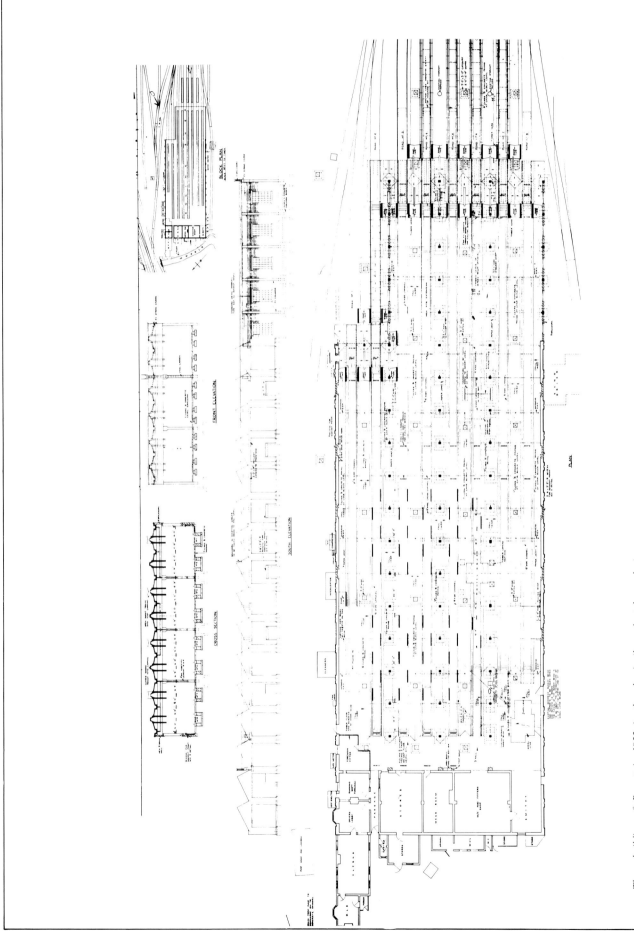

BLOCK PLAN

FRONT ELEVATION

SOUTH ELEVATION

CROSS SECTION

PLAN

The rebuilding of Bescot in 1952 in the classic 'louvre' style made it indistinguishable from sheds similarly dealt with by the LMS, the contract had been issued in April 1951 to Edward Wood & Sons Ltd of Derby, for 'renewal of the roof, pits and pavings'.

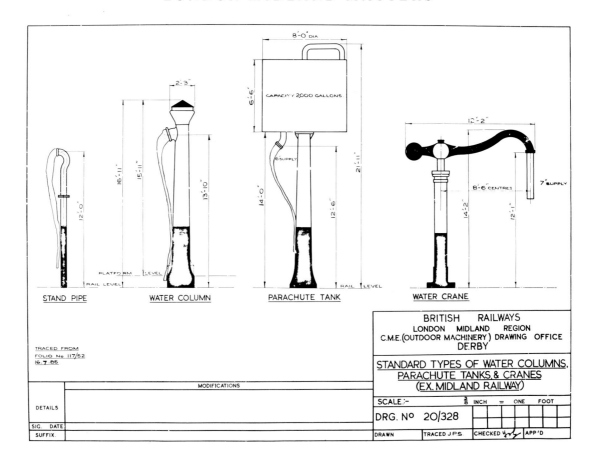

STAND PIPE   WATER COLUMN   PARACHUTE TANK   WATER CRANE

TRACED FROM
FOLIO No 117/52
16.7.86

MODIFICATIONS

DETAILS

SIG.   DATE

SUFFIX

BRITISH RAILWAYS
LONDON MIDLAND REGION
C.M.E.(OUTDOOR MACHINERY) DRAWING OFFICE
DERBY

STANDARD TYPES OF WATER COLUMNS,
PARACHUTE TANKS, & CRANES
(EX. MIDLAND RAILWAY)

SCALE:-   ⅜ INCH = ONE FOOT

DRG. No 20/328

DRAWN   TRACED J.P.S.   CHECKED   APP'D

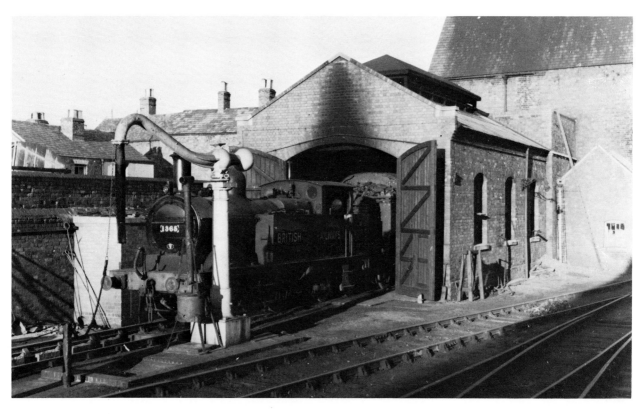

Midland column, with 'fire devil', at Tewkesbury on 10th September 1950.

W.A.Camwell

36

Whilst the water softening plants were indications of a drive to efficiency and economy, harnessing the latest scientific and technical advances, like so much to do with the steam locomotive there was copious (and usually fairly obnoxious) waste generated. The salts dissolved in water from many sources are those harmful to the operation of the steam locomotive. They come out of solution - precipitate - in the boiler much as 'fur' in kettles and 'softening' essentially means removing them before the water is boiled in the locomotive. They appear as a slurry or sludge after chemical 'binding' through other agents. In this waste, semi solid form, it must then be removed from the site. On the steam railway this meant a variety of makeshift vehicles; old tenders were ideal but spillage was inevitable and it characteristically lay all about the softening plant, hardening in fine weather and a clinging fine mud in the wet. These are the 'sludge carriers' at Monument Lane shed, Birmingham, tucked around the side by four raised roads known as *The Promenade*. It was a general dumping ground for stock and stopped engines and featured another perennial water softening feature *The Attendant*. Often a 'medical' case, he usually had sole reign in and about the plant, its technical peculiarities lending the job something of a *mystique*. The Monument Lane man, like most others, was left to his own devices and the water softener remained a mystery to most crews.

W.A. Camwell

Identical column in more cosmopolitan location. Cricklewood c.1928.

Collection Roger Carpenter

5. WAR, OIL & TOIL.

'Epic Story' to unwanted oil

'The Second Phase' of this story of LMS engine sheds occupies the darksome years of the Second World War. It is an arbitrary boundary in a sense - some 1930s projects continued to a conclusion, like Carnforth; others continued in modified or delayed form (Polmadie, Leicester, Upperby) and many were cancelled, like Longsight. Many things failed because of the War but other developments took place that otherwise might not have been. One thing was certain, from 1939 to 1945 the LMS, its Running Department, engine sheds and for that matter the entire British people, were wholly and absolutely changed.

'The Second Phase' of engine shed development upon the LMS saw a variety of resuscitated and rearranged plans and sundry emergency work, ending in some general debacles in the two or three years following War's end. In the *Most Secret* account of the Operating Department's exploits in the Second World War, T.W. Royle (the Chief Operating Manager) contributed a Foreword, issued in March 1943. From 'Watford HQ' (to where the offices had decamped from Euston upon the outbreak of hostilities) he wrote this:

FOREWORD.

During the war, the railways as a whole were subjected to a considerable amount of criticism, and damaging statements were made from time to time in influential circles by people whose sense of responsibility was not always equal to their sense of privilege.

Much of the criticism was due to lack of knowledge of the facts, but it came at a time when the railways were not in a position to defend themselves because they were such an integral part of the war effort that the disclosure of information on any phase of their activities might have divulged something of use to the enemy. Thus, for security reasons, their work had to be carried on under a veil of secrecy.

There was so much that did not come under the public eye, and the individual could know little of the magnitude of the task, or of operational difficulties and the manner in which they were faced.

I, therefore, considered it desirable to have placed on record the conditions under which the Operating Department of the London Midland and Scottish Railway had to perform its war-time task, something of the problems encountered and the technique adopted to overcome them, and to set down some facts as to what was accomplished.

The record will also serve as a valuable historical account of a period unprecedented in the annals of the railway.

It is an epic story, and the nature and scope of the Department's effort in the national cause was so vast that in compiling this record a rigid selection has had to be maintained in order to keep the story within manageable limits and yet do justice to the extent and variety of the subject.

WATFORD, H.Q.
MARCH, 1943.

T.W. ROYLE,
CHIEF OPERATING MANAGER.

Gloom at Camden.

Courtesy Railway Gazette

5. WAR, OIL AND TOIL

Enter the State

'The policy of the LMS since 1923' it was declared 'had been to eliminate wasteful and unnecessary locomotive types by a programme of standardisation and more intensive utilisation, with the object of attaining an ideal stock representing the minimum number of locomotives of standard and powerful types necessary for the efficient running of the line'. This had already proceeded down the two abruptly reversed courses of Horwich and Derby and by 1939 'standardisation' in the sense of a majority of closely related engines, enjoying interchangable parts, had yet to take firm hold. Nevertheless progress had been dramatic:

Year	No. of types of steam locomotives (including diesel, railmotor etc. units)	Total stock of locomotives
1929	287	9829
1930	268	9348
1931	256	9059
1932	224	8477
1933	213	8251
1934	199	8029
1935	183	7906
1936	171	7703
1937	156	7696
1938	151	7655
1939 (Sept)	148	7597

Decrease on 1929 - 2,232

22.70%

The most dramatic falls had come in the Depression years, through a downturn in traffic but it remained demonstrably a praiseworthy achievement - *therefore when war arrived the Co. possessed a locomotive stock which although sound economically judged by peace-time standards could not be expected to embrace without a strain the abnormal demands of wartime traffic.* Government demands for locomotives would be inevitable and was viewed glumly; new construction in the months prior to Prime Minister Chamberlain's wireless declaration of 3rd September had been given over in part to the production of munitions and an acute shortage of labour and materials immediately set in. *At the outset the Chief Operating Manager quickly realised that the utmost use of the existing stock would have to be obtained if the LMS were to fulfil its part in the transport challenges of the country and it was due to his foresight and energetic direction that the locomotive position was able to deal so successfully with the astounding demands placed upon it and which it did so well to withstand.*

All four railway companies made attempts to resist Government requisition of locomotives for they perceived the peril in losing them just when demand would spiral upwards. The War Office had met with the railway companies in July 1939 when 'an estimate of 800 engines within twelve months was advanced as the initial need'. The companies were aghast: *'Whilst it must be evident that to supply such a number from the collective stocks of the railway was remotely beyond the bounds of practicability the problem of finding even a small number for transfer to the military was not one that could easily be solved. It was impracticable to release any engines from the LMS effective stock and likewise as it transpired none of the other companies could offer assistance from their stocks in use'.* The War Office was urged to consider the immediate building of new engines to meet overseas requirements. The capacity did not exist and plans were evolved (responsibility passing to the Minstry of Supply) for the requisition of 100 locomotives of one sort, to facilitate maintenance and repair. It was the Dean 0-6-0 of the GWR which was chosen of course and the LMS contribution to the burden was determined at 40 engines 'and for reasons similar to those which induced the decision to supply locomotives of a single type for military purposes, the engines transferred to the GW company were all of the Class 2 (ex Midland Railway) (0-6-0) freight tender type.' All had to be withdrawn from traffic and to replace these engines it had been in mind to order the rehabilitation of an equivalent number of condemned engines (there was a widespread conviction on the GWR, that they had indeed been

palmed off with the condemned engines but that is another story) In face of 'the excessive arrears in locomotive repairs brought about by much of the capacity of the LMS workshops being engaged in the manufacture of munitions in the months immediately preceding the outbreak of war, the fructification'... (sic?)...'of such a plan could not be expected until a more normal situation had been restored in the shops'.

Further demands followed from the military to which the companies were grimly reconciled .. 'in the face of these overriding circumstances'. 300 ROD 2-8-0s would be required in France it was determined, 250 from the LNER and 50 from the GWR, the LMS undertaking to provide 120 of its 0-8-0s as its share, to be used in place of the RODs on the other two companies. 'The withdrawal of the British Expeditionary Force from France' i.e. the flight from Dunkirk 'automatically cancelled the arrangement'. By June 1940 nevertheless the number of LMS engines 'lost' had risen to 64. In addition to the forty class 2 0-6-0s loaned to the Great Western, eight standard 3F tanks and eight of the precious 350 hp diesel shunters had been lost in France, whilst six former Midland 3F tanks were on the Melbourne Military Railway and two further diesels were 'with the War Department'.

By December 1942 LMS engines 'surrendered to Government Requisitioning' stood at 141 which included 50 or more of the invaluable 8F 2-8-0s 'for the Iranian railways' an order emanating from the War Cabinet which 'overrode any railway considerations' (this has a Churchillian air about it). The engines were necessary to supply the Soviet Union following deep thrusts by German Army Groups into the Caucasus and their loss brought considerable trials. Not only had work to be undertaken 'forthwith and irrespective of any effect on railway operation' for conversion of the 8Fs to oil burning but WD 2-8-0s on loan had also to be rendered up and these in turn had to be restored to original condition. It made for a considerable dislocation in freight working on the LMS; engines of lesser power had necessarily to take over the work, train lengths were reduced and the highly inconvenient backlog was only cleared by extra weekend efforts. On one Division thirty additional trains became necessary *every week* upon the withdrawal of twenty 8Fs. Specials on the LMS by this time merely in connection with armed forces personnel supplies and equipment, let alone the increased demands of industry ran at nearly a hundred *every day..*

At this point .. having demonstrated that the locomotive stock at the outbreak of war was based on peacetime requirements and during the war had receded although the movement of a vastly increased traffic had been accomplished the question will naturally be asked: How was it done?

The problem was solved by the untiring efforts of the Chief Operating Manager in concentrating upon obtaining maximum availability and utilisation of the motive power resources. Numerous expedients were adopted to this end the most important of which were:-

1. Engines kept in traffic for longer periods between examinations

2. Reduction of number of engines under repair

3. Concentration of stocks of spare parts at Motive Power Depots on a more liberal basis

4. Installation of improved running line accommodation and servicing facilities at Motive Power Depots

5. Increased hours of artisan staff at Motive Power Depots and increased hours of female labour

6. Review of locomotive traffic requirements and re-allocation to obtain maximum utilisation

7. Use of the smallest passenger and freight engines to the utmost to release higher powered engines for more important work

8. Deceleration of passenger train services to enable smaller engines to take over the work of larger engines

9. Pooling of inter-railway motive power resources at contact points.

The above was accomplished with a (necessary) ruthlessness which eclipsed Lemon's earlier cost reducing drives; prescribed periods and specified mileages were simply extended, repair times at main works were cut and many more spare parts (turning the 'Concentration' Scheme on its head) were distributed to the sheds which began to take on work previously not contemplated. 'A thorough investigation was made over the whole system to ensure that every available engine however old or small in power was employed to the utmost. Veteran engines which but for the war would have been broken up were kept in traffic and small types employed on light duties were put to work on rural or branch line services in order to release by a process of 'stepping up' the higher powered units for more important tasks'. Amongst the neatest example of this was put in practice on the London Tilbury and Southend section where all the powerful three cylinder 2-6-4Ts were withdrawn for freight work elsewhere and elderly class 3 4-4-2Ts restored to the passenger traffic, involving a deceleration of 3l trains at an average of 3 minutes each. A similar exercise took place on the Rugby-Market Harborough-Peterborough section and elsewhere, to some considerable consternation at the sheds, where the necessary conjuring and juggling with engines in relatively poor condition ('though lets not be prissy about it - they were clapped out') had to be performed. Three instances (what would now be termed 'cascading of units') of the ruses forced upon the LMS are of great interest; there must have been a multitude of such instances and it failed to remedy one of the most frustrating aspects: *Attention was drawn to the continued deterioration of the locomotive repair position on the LMS and LNER systems. Under the strain of intensive working, the number of engine failures on the LMS had increased. The position appeared ominous and to enable the shops to concentrate on repair work in order to reduce the index to a more normal position, the LMS had with reluctance to suspend its building programme. This meant that 36 engines outstanding on the 1942*

Class 4 0-6-0 freight tender engines to Class 5 4-6-0 mixed traffic duties
Class 5 4-6-0 mixed traffic engine to Class 8 2-8-0 freight tender duties

This is a typical case of a little tank engine 'doing its bit' in releasing a big 2-8-0 for vital freight train work.

(c) The work of a Class 2 0-6-2 freight tank engine approximately 60 years of age at Llandudno Junction was adjusted so that it could cover the duties of Class 3 passenger tank engine. The latter was sent to the Wigan area where it acquired a Class 4 passenger tank engine's job enabling this engine to be employed on banking work in place of a Class 0-8-0 freight tender engine which was transferred to freight train working.

Now all this highly necessary wartime expedience had an elegance to it, though its purpose was only dimly perceived at shed level. The partial curtailment of dining car services in 1941 even tempted the authorities to replace Jubilee and Royal Scot 4-6-0s on the consequently lighter trains by Class 4 4-4-0s. The 4-6-0s were then released for the grinding, exhausting work of troop movements but crews and sheds found Compound 4-4-0s on the Euston-Birmingham expresses a trial ... 'they were taxed to such an extent that a means of reducing the load of those already overtaxed trains had to be implemented. This was done by the substitution of modern articulated carriages for some of the

There was an austerity look and feel to most engine sheds, far beyond the Second World War. The bicycle for years had been the only means of travel to and from work and they stood everywhere about most sheds. Generations of gas, steam, water and electric cable pipes laced and threaded the walls and roofing.
Courtesy Railway Magazine

programme could not be completed, and in addition, the programme of 125 engines planned for delivery during 1943 had in the circumstances to be reduced to 99.

Three examples 'of the steps taken to displace powerful locomotives for working freight trains'...

(a) Local passenger trains between Dudley and Dudley Port were discontinued and a Class 1 2-4-2 passenger tank withdrawn. This engine, along with another of the same type was transferred to Bangor where they both worked coupled together on the duties allocated to a Class 3 2-6-2 pasenger tank engine. The Class 3 tank engine went to Rugby where it replaced a Class 4 2-6-4 tank engine which in turn absorbed the work of a Class 4 0-6-0 freight tender engine at Stoke. The Class 4 0-6-0 engine was put on a job schedule for a Class 5 4-6-0 mixed traffic engine thus enabling this valuable general purpose unit to undertake more important work.

(b) An instance of the 'stepping up' process which started at Leeds is demonstrated as follows:

Class 1 0-4-4 passenger tank engine to Class 1 0-6-0 freight tank duties
Class 1 0-6-0 freight tank engine to Class 2 0-6-0 freight tender duties
Class 2 0-6-0 freight tender engine to Class 3 0-6-0 freight tender duties
Class 3 0-6-0 freight tender engine to Class 4 0-6-0 freight tender duties

normal bogie corridor vehicles enabling the total weight of the trains to be reduced.'*

Pooling of resources was another avenue explored to good purpose. A review of servicing arrangements at 'contact points' allowed for some interesting developments. At Abergavenny the LMS took over Great Western shunting work and the LMS freight service between Brynmawr and Abersychan and Talywain was absorbed by the GWR. The LMS was then able to close Blaenavon shed in 1942 'withdrawing two powerful tank engines as well as trainmen and shed staff for transfer to other areas'. The LMS provided an engine to be worked by North Eastern men for shunting at Stafford Common, relieving the latter company of the need to outbase an engine from Derby Fraigrate; shunting at Swansea was co-ordinated and taken over by the LMS allowing a Great Western tank and crews to be reallocated and at Hull two LMS engines were put on LNER train work as 'fill ins' saving the LNER two engines. Coaling began to be undertaken at the sheds of former rivals and repairs also - GW engines at Gloucester for instance travelling across Horton Road to the LMS wheeldrop and

---

*(a) (b) & (c) were oft-recounted, not least by the authors themselves Here it is possible to place them in a more meaningful framework.

thereby avoiding a trip to Swindon. Breakdown arrangements were also revised so that cranes and crews covered 'foreign' Districts.

Repair work continued to suffer through this and remained a nagging worry; 'in normal times it is customary at Motive Power Depots to maintain predetermined stocks - which are not allowed to fall below prescribed minima - of the variety of spare parts and materials required for the repair of locomotives of the different types. Prior to hostilities the average time taken to secure replenishment of stocks was approximately two weeks but as time went on - for the same reasons which had influenced the slow rate of production of new locomotives - this had become much extended'.

The shortage of spares and so on resulted in 'the marked rise in the number of engines waiting material at the Running Sheds' and in March 1941, the figure was 207. To remedy this the flow of spare parts and materials from the locomotive workshops was speeded up and a much improved situation was achieved, the number of egines standing for material at the sheds reduced by 84 by the middle part of 1942.

The following figures show the repairs position on the LMS at various stages throughout the war;

	CME		Motive Power Depots	
Date	Number	% of Stock	Number	% of Stock
2nd September 1939	644	8.5	400	5.3
30th December 1939	409	5.5	333	4.5
29th June 1940	369	5.0	345	4.6
28th December 1940	317	4.2	300	4.0
28th June 1941	333	4.4	391	5.2
27th December 1941	341	4.5	238	3.2
27th June 1942	438	5.8	296	3.9
26th December 1942	427	5.7	236	3.1

Despite the difficulties of obtaining labour and materials there were, at the end of 1941, 465 *fewer* locomotives under or awaiting repair and thus available for traffic compared with the position at the outbreak of war. 'This is the measure of success which attended the Chief Operating Manager's drive, with the ready co-operation of the Chief Mechanical Engineer in the workshops, to keep as many units at work as possible. Unfortunately at the end of 1942 there had been a slight falling away due to circumstances in the workshops but even so there were 381 fewer locomotives out of action than when war broke out.'

It is said that comparisons are odious but the following statistics of the number of locomotives under or awaiting repair on the four main line railways at the 26th December 1942 are of interest:

	CME shops		Motive Power Depots	
	Number	*% of stock*	*Number*	*% of stock*
LMS	*425*	*5.6*	*235*	*3.1*
LNE	*456*	*7.2*	*620*	*9.8*
GW	*260*	*6.6*	*272*	*6.9*
SR	*84*	*4.7*	*94*	*5.3*

The LMS War Report is peppered with reverential verdicts upon the boundless qualities of the General Manager, such that he must have regretted its 'Most Secret' classification. With regard to the 'odious comparisons' relished in the text, it continues: 'The favourable position on the LMS Railway particularly at the Motive Power Depots, will be noted and this provides ample proof of the Chief Operating Manager's wisdom in concentrating on the expeditious repairs of locomotives'.

Cutting Red Tape - 'the Block Grant'

Amongst the practical effects of the conflict were felt at the sheds almost immediately, as lighting in and about the buildings was strictly curtailed. This alone made for serious difficulties and whole shifts were rearranged for work (where possible) to be carried out in daylight. Increased traffic problems with weather, coal and general shortage of staff ('youths of seventeen were put on firing duties under the supervision of specially appointed inspectors') soon exposed the

deficiencies in shed amenities and layouts but a programme of remedial work did not really get under way until 1942. This was after America had entered the war and thus the LMS work formed part essentially of the first stirrings for the Invasion of Europe. Sir Ernest Lemon and his contempories were 'given the nod' by Government throughout 1942 and 1943; the humble 'Second Phase' of the LMS shed story had been officially launched by Lemon on 18th December 1941. The 'Arcadia' conference had began in the days before this, Churchill and Roosevelt agreeing in Washington on a 'Germany First' offensive policy. Back in London Lemon declared to his Traffic Committee that 'Arising out of a review of the circumstances at each of the Company's Motive Power Depots, it is considered that the disposal etc. of engines could be speeded up and the availability increased by approximately 150 engines hours/day by the provision of improved accommodation e.g. additional crossovers, ashpits, watering etc. at the following 26 depots, estimated cost £22,261:*

Motive Power Depot	Cost £	Motive Power Depot	Cost £
Aintree	455	Agecroft	50
Bath	50	Birkenhead	1470
Bletchley	245	Burton	796
Carlisle (Upperby)	3400	Chester	2860
Coalville	395	Crewe South	2630
Derby	1920	Gloucester	445
Leeds Holbeck	130	Leicester	365
Northampton	700	Rowsley	1050
Saltley	100	Shrewsbury	1045
Stockport	555	Warrington	400
Westhouses	215	mmmm	mmmm

Time pressed and the question of whether such expenditure should be submitted to the Ministry of War Transport for Government cash as essential war measures was simply postponed and after further discussion the President (Lemon) simply recommended a block grant (a sort of fighting fund) of £50,000 'to cover these and other schemes' Progress reports were to be made at quarterly intervals.

By June 1942 two further sheds had been added - Bristol (new crossover £2,341 and Dawsholm (additional ash wagon siding £262) to give 28 projects in various stages: 'Gloucester and Northampton are complete, work is advanced at ten. Commencement is to be made at six others, four of them Bletchley, Leicester, Northampton and Stockport have been agreed by the Ministry of War Transport as works fully justified by reason of wartime conditions and therefore paid by the Government'.

All this gathered apace and though most of it was eventually assimilated as 'war work' and thus a charge upon the Government it was nevertheless a very praiseworthy leap in the dark (or at least the gathering gloom) by the LMS; when Lemon launched the crash programme he had no *guarantee* of recompense. On 8th April 1942 W.E. Wood wrote to the Ministry of War Transport from the LMS 'bunker' at Watford: *In order to increase the availability of locomotives we are improving the accommodation at certain of our Motive Power Depots. The bulk of the work will be of a permanent nature and this is being proceeded with as quickly as possible, but work at four Depots costing £1565 would only be required for the period of the war and would therefore be solely to facilitate working of wartime traffic. It embraces the provision of new ashpits/water columns etc and the provision of new and alteration of existing sidings. Will you ascertain from the Ministry of War Transport if this work will be regarded as an MWT scheme? If so I will arrange for proposals to be submitted in the usual way.* The Ministry duly approved, in April 1942, Lt. Col. Mount, C.B. CBE noting in an internal memorandum: *it transpires that the LMS Board have authorised a block grant afterwards referred to as the b.g. of £50,000 for locomotive sheds for war work.*

By September, with the Northern Division obviously ready for a share of the *largesse* further inroads had been made into 'the b.g.' - additional water hydrants at Polmadie (£90), new connection at Stranraer (£375), new connection to the turntable at Dumfries (£400),

On the notepaper the 'Euston' heading is crudely overstamped by 'Watford Temporary HQ'.

4F No.4585, one of the LMS engines converted to oil burning, at Derby on 26th October 1947. The final numbers of such locomotives were out of all proportion to the number of fuelling plants embarked upon and the handful of 4Fs appear to have been the last London Midland engines converted back to coal. 'Some 8F and 5MT' locomotives were 'in hand' the Motive Power Committee declared, as the summer of 1948 waned and on 1st November it was 'reported, the complete cessation of oil burning in locomotives'.

W.L.Good, courtesy W.T.Stubbs.

connecting hydrants 'at Perth(S) shop, (something of the elementary about this - £56), ash lifting at Inverness (£605) and an astonishing £5,380 at Perth for 'a new outgoing road'. By this time thirty schemes had been authorised 'totalling £23,369' (though the sums rarely add up) and the following already brought into use:

Ardrossan	Westhouses
Aviemore	Burton
Canklow	Crewe South
Dawsholm	Derby
Leeds	Rowsley

The work in seven other schemes has now reached an advanced stage.

On 24th June 1943 forty three schemes were reported authorised at a cost of £37,569, the latest brought into use being:

Aintree	Hasland
Sowerby Bridge	Stockport
Dumfries	Chester

making a total of thirty one completed. Three more authorised - St. Rollox (extenson of ash pit) Hurlford (two ash pits) and Ayr (ash pit) brought the total to £41,298. Only days later on 28th June 'several other schemes' were reported complete: Speke Junction (triangle for engine turning and additional ashpit £4,000), Inverness (additional ashpit and conversion of innermost road in shed to dead end siding £760), Millhouses (new ash wagon road and repairs to ash pit £900), Sutton Oak (substitution of water column by water crane to feed four roads £225), Forres (connecting engine road with coal back road and new ashpit £1,000). *Of the schemes referred to in previous reports that at Birkenhead has now been agreed with the GWR as a joint scheme and will therefore not be associated with the block grant. Since the last report improved facilities have been brought into operation at following depots:*

Agecroft	Leicester
Bath	Polmadie
Bletchley	Stourton
Coalville	Warrington

From the foregoing it is clear that war work under 'the b.g.' trickled, poured and finally cascaded into every corner of the LMS. In June 1945, weeks after the Victory in Europe the block grant had been

doubled to £100,000; there would presumably be no Government monies forthcoming for this but the work had a clear value in itself and would become even more starkly necessary in the lean post war years. By 28th November 1945 the total stood at 63 schemes - Saltley (new lines) and Cricklewood (new ash pit) had been approved that day and a further four brought officially into service - Hellifield, Kentish Town, Springs Branch and Motherwell.

Fifty seven of the schemes have been completed the War Minutes end.

OIL

The oft-recalled oil fuel debacle made itself felt across most of the LMS with the exception it would seem of Scotland. It is difficult now to plot the installations; for every example completed there were several where only a start was made and others were adapted or demolished. Those known to have been built (and there will be others) include:

Swansea	Wakefield
Shrewsbury	Newton Heath
Nuneaton	Kirkby-in-Ashfield
Northampton	Nottingham
Crewe South	Mirfield
Wellingborough	Aintree
Toton	Lostock Hall
Stourton	Bath
Normanton	Willesden
Cricklewood	
Westhouses (the bases at least were visible in the 1970s)	

The Railway Observer of 1949 provides a useful summary

Oil Burning Locomotives

The following is extracted from the Comptroller and Auditor-General's Report on the Civil Appropriation Accounts 1947/8. The scheme announced by the Ministry of Fuel in 1946 to convert 1200 locomotives to oil burning was aimed at saving a million tons of coal per year. Expenditure in 1946/7 reached £268,650 and in 1947/8 £1,335,309. In September 1947 when 93 locomotives had been or were being converted, the Ministry of Transport was warned that the 840,000 tons of oil needed annually might not be available. Work on locomotives was suspended but storage depots were completed.

The British Transport Commission told the Ministry that the additional cost of operatng the 93 converted locomotives was £279,000 a year; for the full programme the extra cost would be more than £3½ million a year. Disagreeing with the Ministry, the Commission maintained that extra expenditure on the scheme was not justified. In May 1948 it was abandoned. The 93 oil burners are being reconverted to coal at a cost of £200 each. Expenditure estimated initially at £11,000 and afterwards £10,000 a year is being incurred by the Ministry on care and maintenance of the storage depots. The Ministry in November 1948 estimated its total expenditure at nearly £3 million.

A compaign has been launched to aim at reducing the BR coal bill which amounted to £36 million in 1948 for l5 million tons of coal used. It is stated that coal consumption per mile has risen by 25 per cent over the pre-war figure.

The GWR started its own scheme to convert locomotives to oil burning and four engines were treated in 1945 with another ten converted in 1946.

LMS locomotives converted to oil burning:
l946 2-8-0 C1 8F 8696.
l947 4-6-0 C1 5   4826, 4827, 4829, 4830, 4844.
*   2-8-0 C1 8F 8064, 8079, 8191, 8269, 8273, 8370, 8385, 8386, 8606, 8853.*
*   0-8-0 C1 7F 9511, 9533, 9613, 9642, 9670.*
*   0-6-0 C1 4F 4466, 4552, 4585, 4598.*

0-8-0 9511 was the last engine to be converted back to coal burning, this being carried out in the summer of 1948. The other 0-8-0s were not so treated and were withdrawn in July 1948 at their home shed Wakefield. The newly constituted British Railways conference of Motive Power

Officers heard about it officially at their meeting of 22nd June 1948:

'The Decision of the Executive, 7th June 1948, that all installation work should cease and all Civil Engineering work, other than completion of the buildings to make them watertight for storage of equipment, shall be brought to a close'. In the following July came this item:

Reported, proposal that all oil burning locomotives, with certain exceptions mentioned below, should be stored serviceable at the conclusion of the summer traffic: further instructions in connection with this matter to be issued in due course.

The 'Castle' class 4-6-0 locomotives (WR) and Class 5 4-6-0 Mixed Traffic locomotives (LMR) at present on oil fuel will be converted to coal firing immediately any of them require repairs in the Main Works or at the end of the summer season, whichever is the earlier. Any other locomomotives at present standing out of traffic awaiting repairs on the Main Works, or any others which may become stopped for Shops between now and the end of the summer traffic may also be converted to coal firing when undergoing repairs in the Main Works.

Representations were made by the Southern Region that their main line locomotives fitted for oil burning, viz., 1 'West Country' and 5 N.15/A ('King Arthur Class') should be reconverted to coal burning. In regard to the former, this cannot now be used to good advantage as an oil burner.

Recommended: that this 'West Country' locomotive should be reconverted at earliest possible opportunity; and the 'King Arthur' locomotives reconverted as they go through the shops in the ordinary way, or, if not being shopped in the near future, to be dealt with specially.

Reported: that applications are being received from various sources to acquire the tanks provided under the Coal-Oil Conversion Schemes, and understood the matter of taking up the track at such installations is being raised with a view to assisting the Engineers relaying programme.

The shape of things to come **was raised up at Leicester towards the end of the Second World War. 'Gloriously new,'it was a startling change from existing buildings; 'sectionalised prefabricated concrete' units were used, the whole fitting together in a carefully determined sequence.**

National Railway Museum

Above
Each part of the Leicester roundhouse was pre-cast and pre-tensioned, probably at Newton Heath concrete works. Principal components were the uprights, of course, the inner and outer 'circles' and the radiating beams termed 'cranked cantilevers'. One is visible to the left of the crane (hired out to the contractors at a profit by the LMS) Possessing both lightness and strength each one was lowered and slotted into its support by the attendant crane. Construction, it can be seen, thus had to progress rather like the hand of a clock with each road dug and prepared for the crane to lift the following roof beams into place.
Dorman Long, Courtesy Leicester Museum

Coaling plant under construction in 1953 (the 'Modernization' followed some years after the roundhouse); a contrast with the Midland lower quadrant signal.
Henry Lees & Co.

44

6. 'THE FULL MONTY';
RECONSTRUCTION UNDER BR.
Leicester ('very bad'), Kirkby, Upperby and Crewe - 'Britain's last shed'

Of all the shed design and construction undertaken on BR through the 1950s, most, in the execution of its detail and in the broader principles involved, can be traced in large measure back to the Leicester roundhouse. Thought had long been given to the replacement of the ruinous ex-Midland Railway buildings here and the new Leicester would, but for the coming of War, have proved the culmination of all the 1930s work. It had been a heady period of breathtakingly rapid developments, marvellously telescoped into well under a decade and though the shed itself was not complete until 1945 (with the coal and ash plants following some years later) it represented the final outcome of LMS thinking. The first plans of 1938 had compared straight shed and roundhouse proposals, a final contrast if you like, between the old protaganists of the two building types, the L&NWR and the Midland. Such were the extremes of dereliction suffered at Leicester that rebuildung was contemplated in the most uncertain period of the War; doubtless there would be little need to convince the Ministry of the benefits to working which would be realised.

14th March 1940. Leicester Midland. The Chief Operating Manager reported that those buildings comprising the Leicester Motive Power Depot are in a very bad condition and that portions of the roofs of the existing sheds have to be moved in the interests of safety. In addition the layout of the depot is not satisfactory.

In order to put matters on a proper footing, it is recommended that the depot be modernized, at a total cost of £111,926, principal works being:

(a) Provision of a new shed of octagonal shape with central turntable 70ft. in diameter and 32 radiating roads.
(b) Remodelling of yard layout.
(c) Provision of mechanical coaling plant which will enable 10 coalmen to be dispensed with.
(d) Provision of mechanical ash lifting plant, which will enable 3 ashfillers to be dispensed with.
(e) Provision of new water tank of 75,000 gallon capacity and 6 new water columns.
(f) Electric lighting throughout the premises (existing lighting is by gas) and
(g) Additional and improved office accommodation and staff amenities, stores and fitting shop.

It is estimated that the carrying out of the scheme will result ultimately in increased annual charges of £637 but this does not take into account the saving in time to be effected in the complete disposal of engines which, it is anticipated, will be approximately 1hr/engine, as compared with upwards of 2hrs under present circumstances.

'Moving round the clockface' the crane has completed about half the shed. Both Midland roundhouses with a gentle push, had been quickly demolished to make way for the new octagonal building; during this period Leicester as a *Motive Power Depot* hardly functioned and recourse was made to all manner of organisational conjuring.

Dorman Long, Cty Leicester Museum

SHUNTERS CABIN

60FT TURNTABLE

75,000 GALLON
WATER TANK

No.3 SHED (To be demolished)

LAMP ROOM

MESSROOM

W. COL

.LP

OFFICE

COALING SHED

WEIGH MACHINE

W. COL

.LP

.LP

UP GOODS

DOWN GOODS

UP PASSENGER

LEICESTER NORTH S.B.

From Trent and Derby

To Leicester

FOREMAN

SHEAR LEGS

MESS ROOM

WHEEL DROP

OFFICES ETC.

No.2 SHED

No.1 SHED

70FT. TURNTABLE

NEW ENGINE SHED

ENGINE SHED SIDINGS S.B.

SAND

SHUNTERS MESSROOM

*The new Leicester roundhouse in relation to the sheds it replaced. Its
outline in notional.*

W.A.Camwell

Engines in the ancient Leicester roundhouse in the 1930s, before it sank finally into dereliction. The buildings in truth had been obsolescent really by the 1880s, representing the earliest phase of Midland practice. The dangers, as well as the operating disadvantages of such a place are self evident from this photograph; no discretion was available when stopping an engine and it was impossible even to walk around the shed without ducking under buffers and so on. Nevertheless the place was kept scrupulously clean and tidy, recalling the old and ferocious Midland *Rules of Engine Shed Husbandry*: no walking on the turntable boarding (the pit was always covered in the early days) and engines to be stabled precisely under each smoke ventilator.

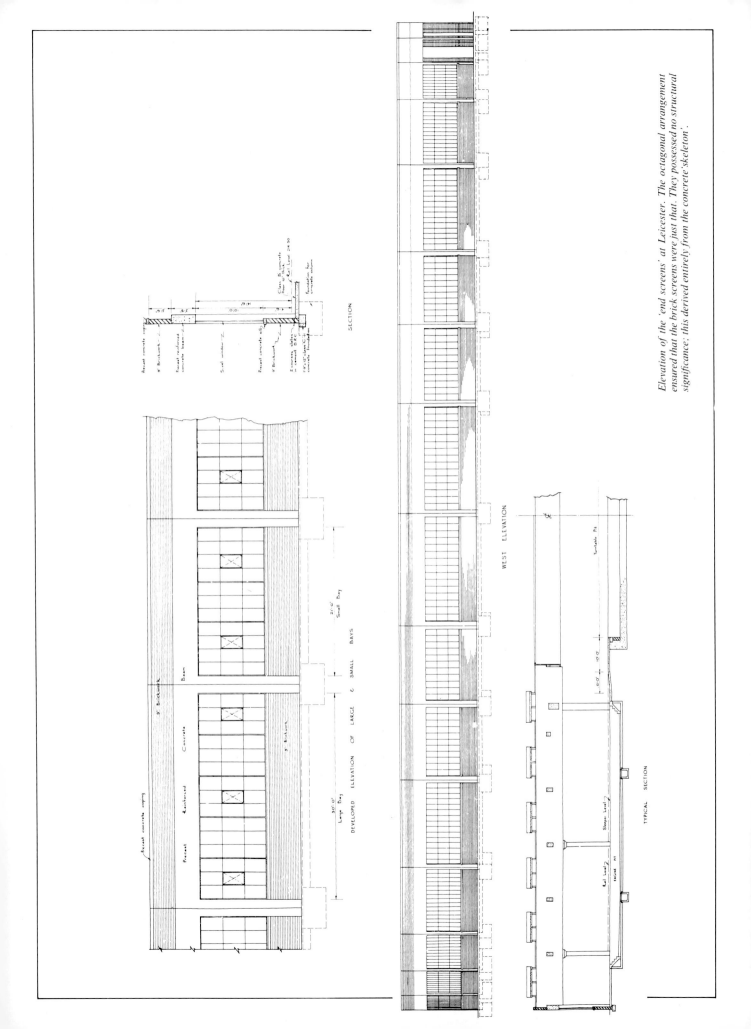

Elevation of the 'end screens' at Leicester. The octagonal arrangement ensured that the brick screens were just that. They possessed no structural significance; this derived entirely from the concrete 'skeleton'.

Elderly Midland 0-6-0, somewhat out of place in the modern roundhouse; it has a tablet catcher and is presumably off an M&GN working. Leicester was long a centre for handling cross country trains, both goods and freight, now long vanished. The lack of buffers was always viewed with some unease at Leicester but the lengthy bays and continuous troughing allowed ample discretion in stopping. The simple brick and glass screens were built indeed with accidents in mind and whilst Upperby suffered at least one such mishap it is not thought that any occurred at Leicester.

Collection R.J. Essery

'Looking out' towards the station in 1947. The new roundhouses were a revelation to staff long used to the inconveniences imposed by the old Midland variety. All roads were 'long roads' of course and the open 'well' allowed smoke to dissipate readily. The pits had inset striplights and an 8F or even a 9F could be manoeuvred up and down without worry, using pinch bars to get at successive bits of the motion.

National Railway Museum

'Looking in' from the station end. The right hand (if such a term is valid, in describing a circle) sector was the 'cosy corner' screened off with radial partitions at the side and sliding doors at the front. Here all the heavy fitting (valves and pistons) was carried out particularly in the winter and it was the obvious place to establish a diesel bay for the coming shunters, Type 2s and Peaks.

Dorman Long, Courtesy Leicester Museum

Leicester yard. Teams of shed enginemen moved locos about, principally from the 'ash pits' ('a place to avoid') to the roundhouse for berthing. Leicester occupied a slightly odd position in the 'Concentration' hierarchy (never wholly established on the LMR, let alone BR) in that it was better equipped than Wellingborough, the 'A' shed of the 15 District and it was responsible for the nearby but physically remote ex-Great Central shed in the city. Road deliveries often came to the wrong shed and orders had to specify 'Beal Street' for the roundhouse.

G. Coltas

Coaling and ash plants going up in 1953.

National Railway Museum

'Turn back' engines (up to 36 in a day might arrive at Leicester) awaiting the next duty, on 20th October 1964. Though there were labourers at Leicester to keep much of the place spick and span (often retired drivers who didnt want to give up the chats and cuppas - or the money) this area was generally left to its own devices. Here 'foreign' engines from Saltley, Nuneaton or Rugby would be parked while the crew went for a cup of tea or a pint. 'Poking the fire up a bit' before the trip home left a fairly obvious mess which was thrown into a wagon every so often and quietly disposed of.

G. Coltas

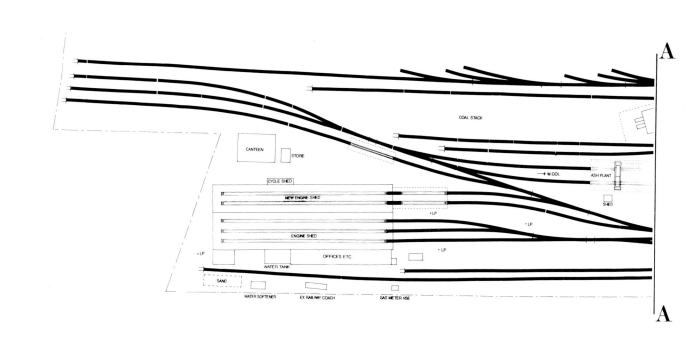

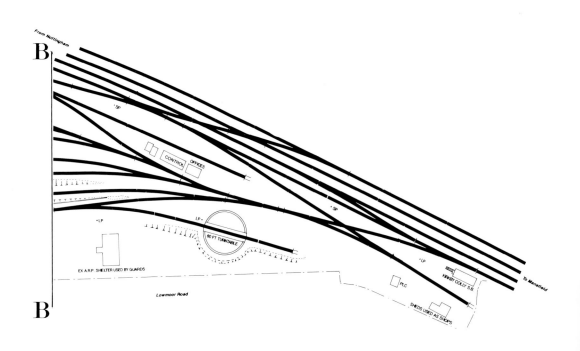

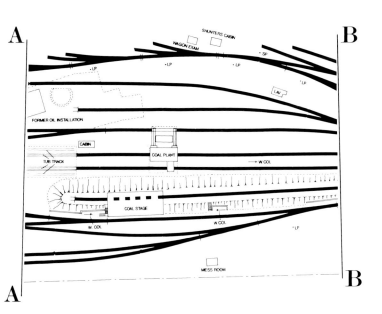

Kirkby in Ashfield - a 'full Monty' project if ever there was one. There was no conception of the rapid demise of steam in 1957 when the project was sanctioned and Kirkby was regarded as the perfect steam shed, working a profitable single traffic (coal) with modern locomotives of relatively few types. Not much more than ten years after it was begun, the whole site was bulldozed wasteland.

Kirkby going up in 1958.

National Railway Museum

The new shed in January 1959. From *The Railway Gazette* **of April 4th 1968 the previous year:** *Kirkby-in-Ashfield Locomotive Depot to be Modernised - Work which has started on the construction of a new mechanical coaling plant at the London Midland Region Kirkby-in-Ashfield locomotive depot.It marks the first stage in a general modernisation scheme for the depot.*

Courtesy Railway Gazette

Inside, the shed was more or less conventional. Concrete for straight sheds seemed to find little favour on the London Midland, though the Eastern and North Eastern continued with it enthusiastically. Sheds like Kirkby, were, it must be said, ugly compared to the roundhouses but they were functional. Old rail, with luck, could even be used for the roof framing, as at Lees near Oldham, and at Nuneaton which was nearing completion as the Kirkby project got under way.

Courtesy Railway Gazette

Midland decoration meets 'fifties brutalism *The Railway Gazette: Other improvements are the installation of electric light in the shed and yard, the provision of additional inspection pits and better signalling. The extension to the shed will afford improved working conditions for the examination and repair of the locomotives based on the depot. Of the 63 allocated, 38 are of the Class '8' freght-tender type.*

Engine Shed Society

Kirkby yard in November 1958. It is not clear if the original Midland turntable was ever changed; it was to be replaced when the first 'Schemes of Modernization' for the depot appeared in 1947. At 60ft it could turn an 8F, and even 9Fs which later arrived but it would have been something of a balancing act, which together with advancing years prompts a suspicion at least that it was something of a trial. It was in any event in the wrong place, 'out on a limb' in relation to the new coal and ash plants. It had long before been the intention to fit it with a vacuum tractor but Kirkby seemed destined to be passed by over the years - the vacuum proposal was abandoned in the early 1930s 'as most of the locomotives here do not possess the vacuum'; it was not so fitted until 1946.

National Railway Museum

The Railway Gazette again: Besides the coaling plant, a mechanical ash lifting plant it to be provided and the engine shed is to be extended to accommodate 32 locomotives instead of 12 as at present. The track layout at the depot sidings is to be remodelled to make for easier working and to improve tight curves which were intended for smaller locomotives than the size now allocated to the depot.

National Railway Museum

Kirkby, New Years Day 1959. Beyond the ash tower is what remains of the Midland coal stage.

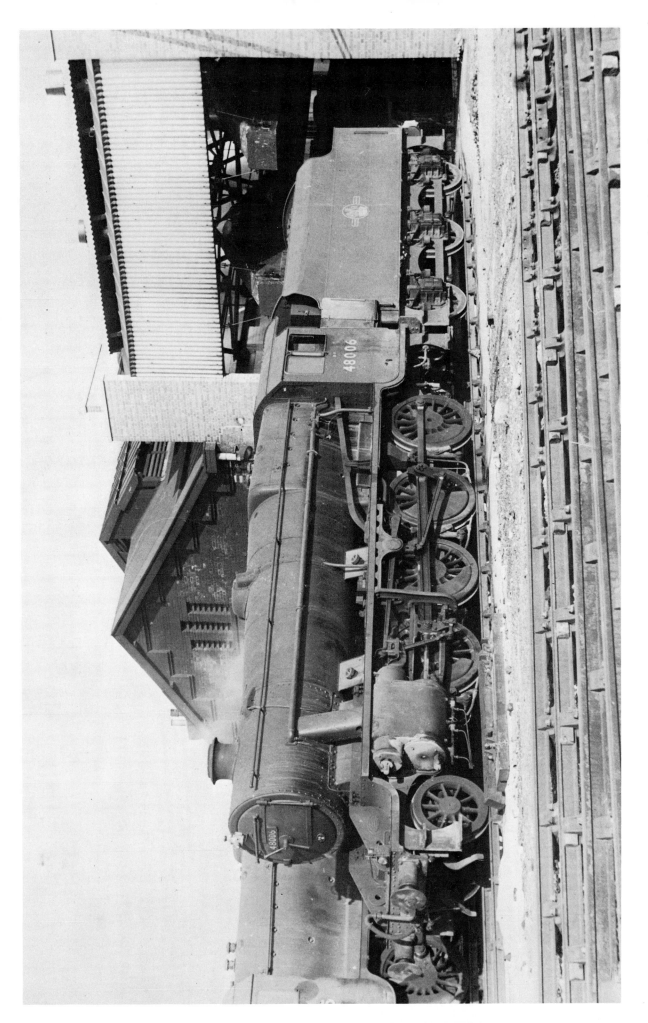

48006 on 5th July 1959. *The locomotives at Kirkby-in-Ashfield are used almost exclusively on working heavy coal trains and the depot is likely to continue to operate with steam locomotives for many years....*
A.R.Goult

Kirkby housed diesels for a while after steam was banished, the new portion of shed retained for their use. It made for an odd sight, the new order amidst the useless relics of the old.

Allan Sommerfield

8F at Kirkby.

Natonal Railway Museum

Carlisle Upperby seems first to have come to the attention ('attention' in this instance indicating the spectre of cash outlay) of the LMS authorities in 1938. On 25th June 'The Chief Officer for Labour and Establishment and The Chief Operating Manager', no less recommended: *that a new staff hostel, with accommodation for 90 men, be provided at Carlisle Upperby in lieu of existing staff hostels at Durranhill (11 men) and Upperby (62men) which are badly sited and much below standard with respect to amenities generally. Estimated cost is £24,164, to be paid under the arrangements of the Agreement with the Treasury dated 30th November 1935 and will form part of the item of £240,000 approved by the Government in respect of staff amenities.*

Now the roof at Upperby, a grand if ancient building of the hipped Ramsbottom type, had progressively fallen into ruin over the ages; it became really an embarrasment, rather after the fashion of Stoke and others.....

28th June 1939. Carlisle Upperby. This shed is a garage under the Kingmoor main depot and deals with most of the engines working to and from the south. At the time of the amalgamation of the railways in 1923 each of the four 'Carlisle' companies embraced in the LMS group had its own Motive Power Depot. Namely:

Caledonian	*Kingmoor*
Maryport & Carlisle	*Currock*
L&NWR	*Upperby*
Midland......................	*Durranhill*

The Maryport & Carlisle Motive Power Depot at Currock was closed in

July 1923 and the Midland depot at Durranhill was temporarily closed in December 1936, the workings being transferred to the Kingmoor and Upperby depots. The Scottish Committee authorised the modernization of Kingmoor depot, at an estimated cost of £28,745, saving £1786 and a new staff hostel. There the Minute ends abruptly and the next references are not found until the deepest War years: *25th September 1941. Upperby. Estimated total outlay was £100,530. Reported that the scheme involved the demolition of the old enginemens hostel, replacement of which was not complete until April last and because of heavy demands on traffic facilities at Carlisle the modernization of the shed has not been proceeded with. Therefore: recommend that the work be postponed until conclusion of hostilities or until such time as circumstances justify a reconsideration.* British Railways completed the Upperby scheme after the War, modelling it on the new Leicester roundhouse (and this is the course presumed to have been charted by the LMS) and what work could be done was executed with this in mind.......*23rd April 1942: the existing 60ft turntable at Upperby is in a bad state of repair due to distortion and corrosion and in the event of a breakdown serious upset to the working at Carlisle would result. Recommended that the 70ft turntable purchased in connection with the modernization scheme at Upperby and now stored at Carlisle be installed in the position it will finally occupy under that scheme, so that in addition to the running on and running off roads three spur roads should also be provided. Cost is estimated at £5,000.*

The roundhouse in 1957, like Leicester its modernisation, the rearrangement of yards and pits came some years after construction of the shed itself.

P. Hitches

The Upperby amenities in 1952. They had seen exhausted crews throughout the war - 'hellish long hours' on endless trip workings. Engines from all over Carlisle were dumped in the adjoining carriage shed yard, sent back dead by the half dozen to Kingmoor, to great consternation. The lobby if all went well, never saw 'foreign' crews from Newton Heath, Polmadie and elsewhere - they were changed over at the station. Problems arose when trains were overloaded - 'a Scot on instead of a Duchess' - and a telephone link was established with Scotland leaving Crewe control somewhat miffed.
National Railway Museum

Corners at Upperby

National Railway Museum

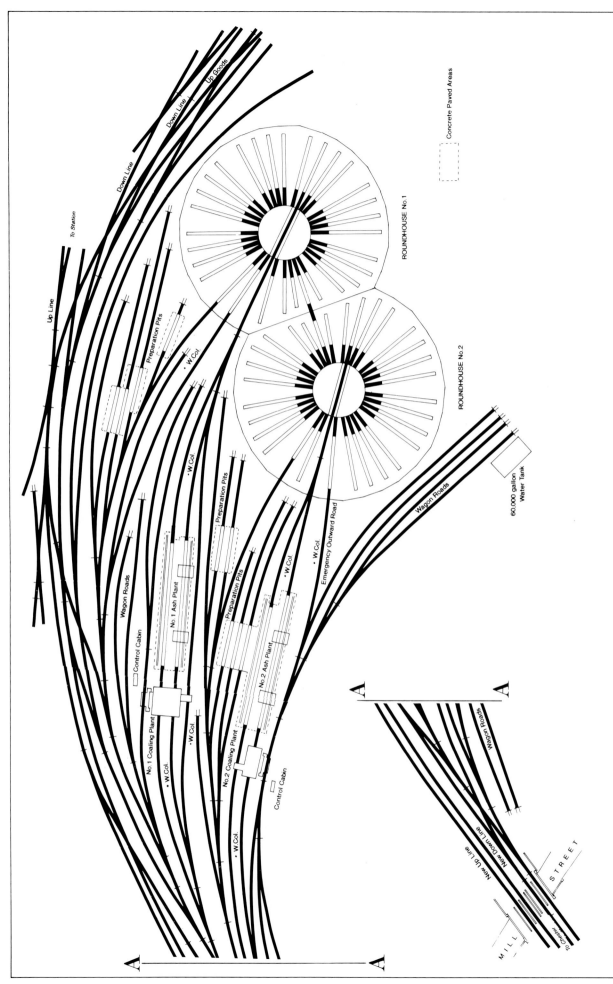

Schemes of great moment were considered by the newly founded BR Motive Power Committee on 22nd April 1948. Doncaster and Langwith were to be rebuilt, taking account of experience recently gained at Polmadie, Glasgow; the new 70ft turntable at Crewe North was noted, 'brought into use 11th April': £195,000 was approved for new works at Southall and the great Thornaby project was inched yet further through the first of its many guises. In addition 'The First Stage' was authorised 'for the Modernization of Crewe North Depot, involving, inter alia, New Coaling Plant, £22,545, Two Ash Plants, £15,866 and 70ft Turntable, £3,993'. BR schemes were increasingly characterised by endless alteration, modification and policy change. Crewe was to have been the culmination of LMS engine shed development, two mighty roundhouses (though at first square buildings were considered) and a modern yard derived from American practice. By the end of the 1950s, altered, curtailed, rethought and cut back, the project had degenerated to a sort of locomotive yard with flimsey 'fan' type of semi roundhouse. This plan represents the proposals at their most grandiose, though the detail varied throughout the 1950s. Only Thornaby, in gestation at the same time, underwent more transmutations; at one time indeed the proposals for it looked very much like this, the great 'might have been' of British engine sheds.

Chaos of rebuilding at Crewe (above) and (left). The new pits and 'table, and coal/ash plants matched the earlier grand ideas but the lightly built semi roundhouse that 'ended the Crewe venture with a whimper' was hardly an advance (in terms of increased accommodation) upon the old ramshackle straight sheds, partly visible in both views.

National Railway Museum

Lancashire Fusilier **at Crewe North on 4th December 1949, with old L&NWR coal and ash plants beyond. 'Urgent action is fast becoming necessary at this place' BR officers reported, within days of Nationalisation. Locomotive work at Crewe indeed had been 'run ragged' by the War; the 70ft turntable at the South shed seems to have been the first of adequate length to have been provided for years; that at Crewe North was hardly suitable and it is not clear how the Pacifics were dealt with. (Though there was a triangle southwards which would bring engines out by the south yard, ready for return to the shed). The L&NWR coal and ash plants were tottering to collapse and the shed buildings were on dire condition.**

E.W.H. Hearst Collection

Mogul 46455 at Crewe, lost amidst the marching ash towers, on 5th October 1952. *W. Potter*

Connaught at the Crewe North ash plant. This form of 'tower' can be regarded as the BR standard. Derived directly from the LMS it largely solved the dismal problem of ash disposal. BR agonised over the messy and dirty, *nineteenth century* nature of ash removal and recognised reluctantly that many small sheds would never have the advantages of mechanisation. It was realised that some hand shovelling would prove necessary everywhere even if only to clear spillage; 'a tarmac' surface was tried but, it was said, somewhat impenetrably,'as with an earth surface there is always digging below ground level....... Blue brick is most desirable although expensive... it is necessary to make the best use of available material under present circumstances, e.g. old boiler plates (in spite of their tendency to buckle and turn up at the corners)'(!).

Authors Collection

Entrance to Crewe North was unprepossessing in the extreme and typical of the huddle of alleys about the ancient shed. It derived from an age when road access, apart from pedestrians, was largely irrelevant.

Gordon Coltas

Ceylon beneath the ash tower. On 18th March 1948 the future of ash plants was discussed; 'the question of using simple or double lifting plants should be determined .. the question of standardisation on agreed types will ultimately have to be considered and the installation at Crewe, now approved by the Executive, as the most up to date available will, it is hoped, provide a basis for comparison.

Collection M. Mehra

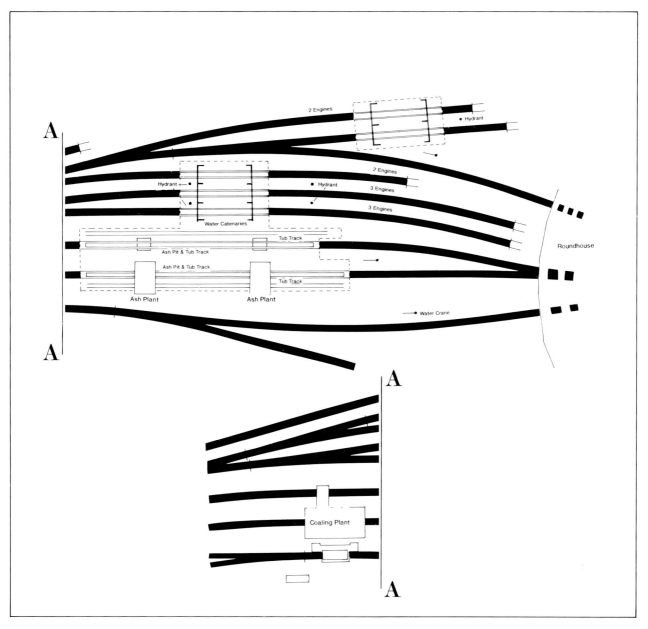

Crewe North finished up much more of a servicing yard than the final expression of engine shed development and overhead delivery systems, pioneered on the LNER in Britain and derived from American practice was to be employed for the first time on the LMR. Ultimately reduced from the two vast roundhouses of page 62 to a rather lightly constructed 'sectored' building, through continuing adjustments to the plan and a reassessment of steam working at Crewe, 'the roundhouse principle' had nevertheless been firmly established in the ascendancy in Britain, for the first time. The following summarised extracts derive from the BR 'shed analysis committee' of the late 1940s which in turn drew upon much of the post-war investigation of the big companies. *Planning of Steam Locomotive Depots* **was issued in March 1952 and set the principles to be followed for the remainder of the decade.** *Thirty six depots were analysed falling into two main groups... eleven depots having sheds of the roundhouse type with one to four turntables, and twenty two depots of the straight shed type, either stump or double-ended. The other three depots comprise one fan type of shed, and two having both roundhouse and straight sheds. The roundhouse shed having stabling roads radiating from a turntable is, from the operational aspect, the better type. The main objection is that, per locomotive berth, the area of covered accommodation is greater than that of the straight shed type. Advantages of a roundhouse type of shed are considerable: they provide greater protection from cold winds than straight sheds; the perimeter wall is continuous, except for the comparatively small archways for the incoming and outgoing roads, whereas the straight shed is open for the entire width of the building, and in a through shed, at both ends. Locomotives may be stabled in any vacant berth, and once stabled there is no further movement required; work can be carried out upon the locomotive without interruption and in safety, and there is no shunting required to marshal the locomotives in order of departure times, as is necessary at straight sheds. The resultant saving in footplate staff is considerable, equal to 3.7 hours driver's and fireman's time per week per engine allocated, that is to say, at a straight shed having 50 engines allocated, four additional sets of footplate staff are employed upon shed duties compared with a roundhouse shed of similar allocation. Comparison of shunting and marshalling times: Straight shed 6.5 hours per week per engine. Round shed 2.8 hours per week per engine.*

The Crewe semi roundhouse under construction in August 1959. It is seen to be entirely different in principle and materials from the big LMS/LMR concrete roundhouses. It looked much like some lost offspring of The Festival of Britain and though wholly unlike other engine sheds in the country it owed much to some contemporary station buildings.

National Railway Museum

'The glasshouse' in October 1959.
J.R.L. Allen

The roundhouse was the architectural version of an afterthought but nevertheless considerable effort and ingenuity went into its design. Whatever the effect of the building on ones sensibilities, it certainly garnered the maximum possible light, from a novel circular northlight roof.

National Railway Museum

44770 outside, in May 1965. The building proved ill suited to the assaults of smoke, blast and weather and was unkempt by the end.
Gordon Coltas

The waters of the 'super shed' at Crewe were further muddied by 'The Examination and Repair Shed'. Valve and piston examinations on LMS Pacifics required specialist attention; in the 1950s sheds such as Crewe, with primitive accommodation, were proving less and less suitable and this building was designed as a radical solution. It would form 'a supplementary concentration depot' and all West Coast Pacifics from Camden to Polmadie would be dealt with here. The engines would be shunted in dead, so no smoke ventilators were needed. It soon struck someone, as the building neared completion in 1958/59, that the cleanliness demanded by the complex work rendered it ideal for diesels. Without seeing a single Duchess (it is believed) the building was eventually commandeered as 'Crewe Diesel Depot'. This building, familiar now for years, with its succeeding generations of Type 2s, 4s and so on, turns out to have been Britain's last engine shed.

Gordon Coltas

The great shed at Wakefield in 1954, built on a modified system which though superficially akin to the earlier LMS system was simpler and thereby cheaper. The concrete louvres gave way to the more conventional 'pots' and the ridges in between were glazed, topped with corrugated sheeting.

National Railway Museum

7. NEW ROOFS (REPRISE).
Goole and others

'Holes in roofs' as we have seen, were all too common (see just one instance, Rose Grove page 15 and below). The LMS in one of its bold strokes determined upon a spirited campaign and the Works Committee duly sanctioned £530,000 on 28th November 1945 for new roofs, lighting pits etc at 28 sheds, from the tiny to the vast. Furthermore the Chief Civil Engineer *had reported that a design for re-roofing the round engine sheds had been agreed and therefore it was recommended that authority be given for renewing the roofs and repairing the pits and paving at the following 13 roundhouse engine sheds:*

Toton   Nos.1 and 2
Belle Vue
Saltley   Nos.1,2 and 3
Cricklewood   Nos.1 and 2
Kentish Town   No.1
Hasland
Wellingborough   No.1
Stourton
Peterborough

The total estimated expenditure for the 41 engine sheds would therefore be £950,000

The scale of the work, with post war shortages of labour and material made for slow progress - only so many sheds could be dealt with in a year; in 1947 alone at least ten projects were 'finalised':

Aintree	£19,933
Goole	£21,206
Lincoln	£4,832
Aston	£27,539
Edge Hill	£27,036
Wakefield	£17,009
Fleetwood	£17,576
Alsager	£7,656
Burton	Unknown
Low Moor	Unknown

These represented just about the last LMS acts with respect to its engine sheds, a programme that had seen enormous effort and money and yet still so much remained to be done. It was small wonder that the subject would be one for BR to return to, again and again.

2nd March 1948....... In view of the serious complaints from staff as to the conditions under which they perform their essential functions owing to the lack of efficient shelter it is necessary that some estimate should be obtained as to the position throughout the country in regard to shed roofs, and the action which being taken to improve the position. The Regional Officers were accordingly requested to prepare statements setting out apparent condition of their shed roofs, i.e. 100% water-tight, 75%, 50% etc., or where without roofs, indicating those cases and dates where the matter has already been reported to the Chief (Civil) Engineer's Department........22nd April 1948. Further to Item 4: the condition of Motive Power Shed roofs was discussed and it was emphasized how in a number of cases the condition of the roofs affects the proper servicing of locomotives, which has its effect on running.

It was ascertained that no less than 233 sheds on BR were '100% watertight' and no less than 93 of them were on the LMR. The London Midland moreover had 22 that were 'over 90% watertight' and 23 (the judging of this must have been a joke) 'over 60% and up to 90% watertight'. Another 19 were 'over 30% and up to 60% watertight' and a miserable 13 were held to be 'up to 30% watertight'.

'Less than 30% watertight' at Rose Grove.

R.K.Coventry

Compound 4-4-0 inside Bedford shed. Sectionalised concrete continued to be used on the London Midland Region, the purely LMS techniques of the 'louvre' having usurped the variety of 'single pitch' designs more characteristic of the 1930s. Steel framed ash plants do not seem to have been put up post war and concrete became *de rigeur* for such items in the 1950s.

Collection Colin Jones

Construction in progress at Bedford. 'This shed has long been overdue for replacement' the Motive Power Officers heard in 1950 and it was estimated that 'its reconstruction might usefully be incorporated into the latter stages of the schemes for renewal of the round sheds'.

National Railway Museum

Bedford under the shadow of its coaling plant.

The rebuilding of Bescot (see plan page 35) took place in 1952 and from the condition of the old L&NWR north-light roof it is not hard to devine why.

Anthony Goodey

The new Bescot. The cutting back of two of the roads enabled some refinement to the track layout and the resulting two road 'short' section is believed to have subsequently been turned over to diesel shunters. Any part of a shed amenable to separation was usually grabbed for this purpose in the 1950s.

National Railway Museum

Transition 13th August 1952.
National Railway Museum

Bescot interior, April 1953. It was one of '28 rectangular engine sheds, approved for the purposes of improving the lighting, renewing the roofs and repairing and renewing the engine pits and paving.....approved expenditure £530,000'(!) In 1948 the Motive Power Committee recorded that 'the condition of our shed roofs, is, in a good many cases, not such to get the best results from the Motive Power staff.' In this they were assuredly correct. The new roofs (see the Bescot forebear opposite) were demonstrable improvements.

Anthony Goodey

New offices, 1956.
Herbert Collins

Sowerby Bridge on 2nd October 1953. It is almost possible to estimate the percentage of its area which might be 'watertight' though the exercise carried out by BR was essentially a pointless one. A bucket is useless with one hole or many.

Frank Harrison

Sowerby Bridge on 21st October 1953; the archetypical 'Lanky' shed, though it was built in stone rather than brick. The bay window of the foreman's office is the most familiar feature, a useful point from which to survey the yard.

Peter Kemmett

The shed like others before it was rebuilt more or less from the ground up, rather than simply 'reroofed'. The techniques of course were almost precisely those of the LMS before, an interlocking network of concrete beaming. 5th April 1954.

National Railway Museum

Whilst Sowerby Bridge, from the front at least (see previous page) was almost respectable in its appearance Goole (above) was rather different. Much of the first part of the roof had been taken down years before by the LMS, possibly bcause of fire and most of the remaining slates had subsequently given way to corrugated sheeting. Goole suffered violent, freezing, gales which sliced through the shed and drifting snow was frequently a problem in winter. Rebuilding was desirable, to say the least.

National Railway Museum

Though Goole could appear gloomy, as in this rather darksome photograph, well tended gardens lined the wall. They were begun by a member of staff, a keen gardener and in the early 1950s Cottingham, the old NER nursery which provided for many stations, on request sent a dozen boxes of plants, which were used to great effect.

National Railway Museum

'The roof off' at Goole in June 1955. The shed was isolated, two miles out of the town and it could only be reached alongside the goods line out of the docks. It was acordingly rather creepy at night, the wind making for some unnerving noises. York Minster was just visible from the coaling plant on a good day and in season cleaners scrumped apples from the adjacent farmland. The old L&Y saddle tanks were mistrusted by the North Eastern Region after takeover in 1956; they were used on the many pilot turns (almost every link had some pilot work within it) but shortly after transfer to the NER the boilersmith managed to pierce the firebox of one of the tanks with a hammer. Though the actual incident may have been rather less apocalyptic than this nevertheless much consternation was apparent at Hull, the depot now responsible for the District and the 'Lankey' engines were banned. They were replaced by two J39 and three J25 0-6-0s and a J72 0-6-0T, the latter proving particularly popular.

National Railway Museum

Volcanic scene at Goole in October 1955. Roads were numbered 1 to 6, left to right and No.1 (see the smoke pots above it) ran less than half the length of the shed. The original offices at the rear were long before given over to fitting work and rather unsatisfactory replacements were provided along the rear part of the erstwhile No.1 road. The pit remained in place and could even be found by lifting the odd floorboard. It was worrying for the occupants, well aware of the stopping powers of an A Class 0-6-0 or a saddle tank and eventually engines were banned from 'No.1' altogether and sleepers piled across the entrance.

National Railway Museum

Goole in August 1955, its new roof nearing completion. The little 2MT mogul, present on road No.2 in many of these photographs, was useful for the Isle of Axholme line - 'it went off in the morning and came back when it was ready - no one really knew what it did.' The WDs characterized much of the workings, clumping endlessly in and out of the District on slow goods 'a bit like slowly wandering large animals on the African plain'. An exotic simile but an effective one.

National Railway Museum.

Goole in November 1955. Its isolation ensured that the bicycle and increasingly the motorbike, remained principal form of access.

National Railway Museum

Goole interior, December 1955. The shed was 'out on a limb' in a L&Y (or LMS) context and was odd for other reasons. It was the only 'Lankey' shed which had no work to Manchester or Blackpool and after 1956 had to order its spares from at least seven works - Crewe, Derby and Horwich for obvious purposes; Doncaster and Darlington for North Eastern Region types, Cowlairs for the J39s and it even had a Swindon maintained WD 2-8-0. There was even an A5 4-6-2T for a while, which conceivably would have added Gorton to the list. Further oddities included three ex-MR lF tanks. They had arrived for pilot work but their open cabs were regarded with some horror; Dairycoates surreptitiously knocked up some steel back cabs, fixtures that were carefully removed before the engines went back to Derby.

Eric Hutchinson

A cold day of wind at Goole, near to Christmas in 1955. At some point, as we have seen, this simpler arrangement of concrete roof usurped the complex LMS 'louvre' system used until the early 1950s.

National Railway Museum

Goole in 1955.

National Railway Museum

8. THINGS DONE....AND UNDONE.

Willesden, one of the great 'undones,' a sprawling 'steam shed' in west London, notable for what it had lost as much as for any improvements. An entire new shed in northlight style had once stood at the front of the old hipped roof building seen here - possibly the only large L&NWR building to be completely erased years before the end of steam. It was also famous for its ill starred 'pneumatic smokebox ash extractor', a device tried to similar negligible effect at the neighbouring Old Oak Common of the GWR. It had been in operation under the supervision of the contractors since 28th January 1933 and 'as a result of the experience gained it should be considered a failure.'

Collection Anthony Goodey

Walsall shed about to 'get the treatment' in 1953. The carefully ordered locomotive springs were in fact stowed to standard patterns, recognisable across different sheds. There were umpteen types and were normally placed with the reference number easily visible.

Engine Shed Society

Holbeck, the classic stage for light and shade and a shed which retained its Midland air to the end.

P.D.Grimshaw

Midland coal stage, unusually executed in wood at Hellifield in 1961. This was another peculiar survivor and owed more to Scottish (where tumbledown wooden stages were abundant) than usual Midland practice.

T.J. Edgington

Steel and Asbestos as applied to Blackpool Central shed in 1958: *Smoke extraction troughs are fitted over the engine roads and the roof covering consists of patent glazing with curved asbestos sheeting at the ridge. The side covering above wall level is of asbestos sheeting.*
L.S. Logan

This account necessarily concentrates on the larger sheds, though a number of smaller buildings were renewed or rebuilt, even Coniston, with slightly absurd results. Overseal, where a Midland shed was conjoined with LNW 'coal hole' was more typical, in that nothing of note occurred, over decades.

A.George

'Full Monty' coal and ash at Birkenhead.

K.R. Coventry

Nuneaton before rebuilding. It was renewed with old rail and sheeting in a similar style to Blackpool (above left) in 1957 - 'New Roof for Nuneaton Engine Shed': *Roof girders made from serviceable secondhand lengths of rail were used by British Railways, London Midland Region, in the renewal of the engine shed roof at Nuneaton motive power depot, work on which is now nearing completion. The old rails were used for the main girders, roof frames, and bracing, after successful experiments with them on other light roof structures of this type. The rails are of an ideal weight and shape for such purposes and are resistant to corrosion. the old roof of the shed was of timber supported by cast-iron columns and brick side walls and had become due for renewal. The new roof consists of two clear spans of 51 ft supported on strengthened side walls and one central row of 11 steel stanchions replacing the previous 55 cast-iron columns. The used rail main girders, roof frames and bracing are fabricated to a standard design.*

R.K. Coventry

Camden, where it can be said, 'much of it started', for it was chosen to illustrate the 1930s *Railway Gazette* '£1m' account and has since been inextricably linked with the London Midland *Modernizations*. It was also famous for its smoke problem and the running battles with the local council. Endless devices were resorted to, including filling one bunker of the coal plant with coke, which was *supposed* to be delivered to the front part of the tender only. This would cut smoke on lighting up but the relative quantities were inevitably wrongly loaded, making for a fraught exit from Euston, firing coke to Tring perhaps, amid much cursing.

R.K. Coventry

Further evidence of the smoke dilemma at Camden.

R.K. Coventry

One of the most protracted schemes was that involving Longsight, with its two vast 'North' and 'South' sheds. The North shed was 'kitted out' in 1948 and the South followed in 1956, the shed effectively being dug up whilst *in situ* if such a thing is possible. *The Railway Gazette* **reported the imminent scheme in its issue of July 8th 1955.:** *Work is to begin shortly on a £100,000 scheme for the reconstruction of the south shed at Longsight motive power depot London Midland Region, including the renewal of the roof, remodelling of the track layout, and renewals of the pits and pavings. An electric wheel drop and electric lighting will be installed with fluorescent lighting in the pits. The roof of the shed will be rebuilt with steel roof beams carrying patent glazing and will have continuous smoke outlets. All the pits inside and outside the shed will be renewed and drainage, water and compressed air services provided. The eight roads will be reduced to six to give wider space between. Opportunity will be taken to raise the rail level to improve the gradient into the shed and a new crossover will be constructed between Nos. 11 and 12 roads. There are two single end sheds at this depot and the present scheme concerns the south shed, the north shed having been re-roofed in 1948. The initial contract for the work has been let to Charles R. Price, Barnsley Road, Doncaster, for the renewal of pits and pavings.*
(Top: 5th March 1956, above: 9th April 1956)

The Railway Gazette

Final round of roofing at Rose Grove.

ACKNOWLEDGEMENTS

This work developed from a desire both to tidy up some loose ends and to open up some dead ends. Some of the detail of the vast technical, scientific and human organisation that was the LMS Running Department is now more clearly seen, we hope, and our understanding taken a bit further. Many of the most enlightening documents, the reports, summaries, tables and diagrams never reached the Public Record. Much of it was lost, dispersed, thrown away, taken home for old times sake. By its nature it was distributed piece meal about the railway and unlike the centrally held Committee Minutes could not be 'called in' when the time came. Holes in the story await the gradual uncovering of these surviving fragments.

London Midland Matters is the third in the series *British Railways Engine Sheds* which began in 1988 with two humble paperbacks, *An LNER Inheritance* and *A Southern Style*. It was a matter of some heart searching to alter the format but well, *it just grew and grew.*

Thanks go to Stephen Summerson, whose notes are constantly worth plundering; to Alec Swain, who can conjure an unusual insight more or less out of the air, to Alan Wilson, for similarly thoughtful analysis; and to Terry Smith and Lawrence Taylor, who kindly recounted with patience and great wit, their LMS and LMR experiences at various places. Enormous thanks are also due to W.A.Camwell, to R.K.Coventry, Peter Hutchinson, Gordon Coltas, A. Davenport, G.Gilbert, Eric Hutchinson, R.J.Essery, Brian Hilton, Eddie Johnson, G.B.Perkins, K. Holden, N.E.Preedy , E.W.H. Hearst, Bill Stubbs who yet again provided that last minute print, the late W.L.Good, M. Mehra, P. Sutcliffe, Colin Jones, Frank Harrison, Bernard Matthews, P. Higginshaw, A.R. Goult, Alan Sommerfield, J.R.L. Allen, W.B. Underwood, Henry Lees & Co., Dorman Long, Mitchell Conveyor & Transporter Co., Yorkshire Post, City of Leicester Museums, National Railway Museum, The Railway Gazette, The Railway Magazine, The Thompson Society, The Engine Shed Society.

The records upon which this book is based are those at the Public Record Office at Kew and to a lesser extent the National Railway Museum. Thanks are especially due to the staff at both these places who cope ably with a daily round of odd requests, and (occasionally) some even odder people.

Thanks also to Beverly, Christine and Wendy, who also cope with some pretty odd people.